Comptroller of the Currency
Administrator of National Banks

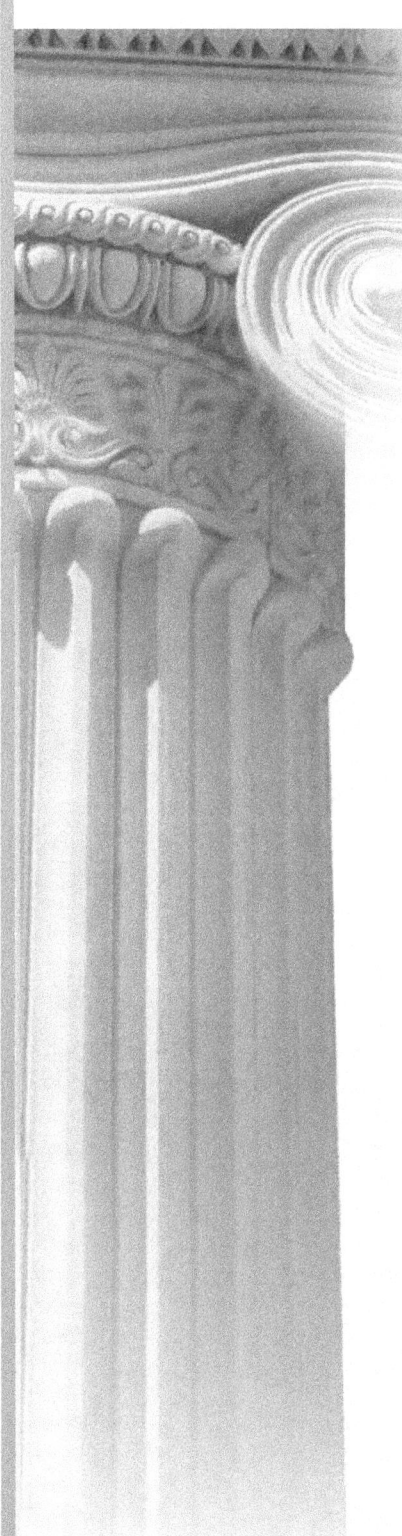

Performance and Accountability Report

FISCAL YEAR 2002

Message from the Comptroller

Figure 1: John D. Hawke, Jr.

I am pleased to present the Office of the Comptroller of the Currency's (OCC) "Performance and Accountability Report" for Fiscal Year (FY) 2002. The performance and financial data presented in this report are fundamentally complete and reliable, as outlined in the guidance provided by the Office of Management and Budget (OMB). The report is based on data contained in the OCC's management information systems and is presented in accordance with accounting principles generally accepted in the United States of America (GAAP).

The OCC is responsible for the licensing, regulation, and supervision of all of the nation's federally chartered (national) banks. The OCC promotes a safe and sound banking system by requiring that national banks adhere to sound banking and management principles and that they comply with laws and regulations. Under the OCC's jurisdiction are approximately 2,100 national banks and 52 federal branches and agencies of foreign banks, representing more than 58 percent ($3.8 trillion) of the total assets of all United States (U.S.) banks.

One of our significant accomplishments during 2002 was the more complete integration of risk-based supervision into supervisory activities and resource allocations. Our supervision process is organized along two lines of business: large banks and mid-size/community banks. We have taken this approach to supervision realizing that institutions of varying sizes and complexity present different risks and require unique supervision philosophies. Risk-based supervision consists of activities to identify, analyze, and respond to emerging systemic risks and trends that could affect an individual national bank or the entire national banking system. As part of this process, analytical tools and models are designed and developed to tailor examination procedures based on risk profiles and to allocate resources accordingly.

The OCC undertook a number of initiatives to respond to the USA PATRIOT Act requirements and the threat of terrorist financing through the national banking system. These initiatives included special reviews of selected banks to evaluate anti-money-laundering (AML) systems, including terrorist financing controls and USA PATRIOT Act compliance. In addition, the OCC updated its AML training to include USA PATRIOT Act requirements and delivered the course to the OCC examiners and foreign bank supervisors. The OCC provided speakers for industry conferences on the subject of AML and the USA PATRIOT Act and participated in U.S. government anti-terrorist financing or AML initiatives involving other countries.

I remain committed to reforming the funding for bank supervision. The current funding arrangement, under which state banks are subsidized by their federal supervisors, is unfair to national banks, which are forced to contribute to the subsidization of their state-chartered competitors while bearing the full cost of their own supervision. It also disrupts the constructive competition between state and federal bank regulators that has been the hallmark of our dual banking system for more than a century. The current arrangement potentially compromises the safety and soundness of all banks. With reform of the deposit insurance system high on the nation's legislative agenda, it is an ideal time to also correct the inequities of funding bank supervision.

In September 2002, we announced a realignment of our district office structure to ensure that our operations are appropriately aligned for the future. We undertook a study to evaluate whether the locations from which, and the means by which, our district office functions are being performed are optimal and best aligned with our long-term supervisory strategy. We expect significant benefits to be realized from this restructuring.

I am fortunate to have the resources of approximately 2,800 dedicated, and extremely professional employees to assist in our mission of supervising, regulating, and chartering national banks. Our accomplishments during the fiscal year were due to their extraordinary efforts. We will continue to find innovative ways to meet our mission using our resources efficiently and effectively. We are ready to meet the challenges that lie ahead in making sure our national banking system is safe, sound, and fully competitive.

John D. Hawke, Jr.
November 15, 2002

Table of Contents

OCC-at-a-Glance

Mission:
The OCC charters, regulates, and supervises national banks to ensure a safe, sound, and competitive national banking system that supports the citizens, communities, and economy of the U.S.

Strategic Goals:
- A safe and sound national banking system,
- A flexible legal and regulatory framework that enables the national banking system to provide a full competitive array of financial services,
- Fair access to financial services and fair treatment of bank customers, and
- An expert, highly motivated and diverse workforce that makes effective use of OCC resources.

Key Components:
- Approximately 2,100 national banks and 52 federal branches of foreign banks
- Approximately 2,800 employees at headquarters, district, and field offices
- Major programs: supervise, charter, regulate, and analyze risk

Condition of National Banks:
National banks registered record earnings in both the first and second quarters of 2002, as low short-term interest rates and wide spreads between short- and long-term rates boosted net interest income. Return on equity continued to rise, approaching the all-time highs recorded in the early 1990s. Both noncurrent loans and provisions for loan losses rose over the previous year, as asset quality continued to drift lower, with most of the deterioration concentrated in the larger banks.

Program Results:
- 3,100 examinations conducted
- 150 formal appeals and inquiries processed
- 330 enforcement actions completed on banks and against individuals
- 170 community development consultations held with bankers
- 75,000 consumer inquiries and complaints opened
- 3,500 corporate applications received
- 30 new national charters approved
- 12 final rules issued
- 115 supervisory issuances and booklets published

OCC-at-a-Glance

Significant Program Accomplishments:

- Assigned dedicated examiners-in-charge for each mid-size bank
- Implemented minimum core examination procedures for low-risk, stable community banks and expanded procedures for institutions exhibiting higher risk
- Responded to the USA PATRIOT Act, by:
  - ⇒ Evaluating AML systems, including terrorist financial controls and USA PATRIOT Act compliance, in selected banks
  - ⇒ Issuing regulations implementing the Act
  - ⇒ Conducting AML training for examiners and foreign bank supervisors
  - ⇒ Providing speakers on AML and the USA PATRIOT Act for industry conferences
  - ⇒ Participating in U.S. Government anti-terrorist financing or AML initiatives involving other countries
- Provided more centralized oversight to problem banks
- Litigated court cases involving preemption of state law by federal law
- Enhanced risk assessment models and tools

Significant Financial Management Accomplishments:

- Implemented a Joint Financial Management Improvement Program (JFMIP) certified financial and acquisitions management system ($MART) on October 1, 2001
- Received an unqualified opinion on the FY 2002 financial statements
- Met Treasury's goal for timely, accurate monthly financial reporting
- Achieved 86 percent of targeted level for reserved funds

Performance Measures:

- Completed quarterly risk assessments on 100 percent of large and mid-size banks
- Issued reports of examination to 97 percent of large and mid-size banks
- Achieved 98 percent compliance with the Federal Deposit Insurance Corporation Improvement Act (FDICIA) mandated examination schedule for community banks, 4 percent more than FY 2001
- Processed 96 percent of corporate applications within timeframes
- Closed customer complaints and consumer inquiries in an average of 44 calendar days
- Improved to "reasonable assurance" on the Federal Managers' Financial Integrity Act (FMFIA) Section 4 and "substantial compliance" on the Federal Financial Management Improvement Act (FFMIA) from previous years
- Exceeded targets for all 10 customer service standards for examinations and licensing services

PART I

MANAGEMENT'S DISCUSSION AND ANALYSIS

Part I – Management's Discussion and Analysis

ORGANIZATIONAL PROFILE AND STRUCTURE

Profile

The OCC was established in 1863, as a bureau of the U.S. Department of the Treasury. The OCC is responsible for licensing, regulating, and supervising the nation's federally chartered banks.

Today, the OCC regulates and supervises approximately 2,100 national banks and 52 federal branches of foreign banks in the United States. National banks account for more than 58 percent of the total assets of all U.S. commercial banks.

The OCC's operations are primarily funded by semiannual assessments levied on national banks and from various licensing fees. The OCC also receives interest revenue from its investments in U.S. Treasury securities.

Structure

During FY 2002, there were approximately 2,800 OCC employees. The OCC is headquartered in Washington, D.C., operates a data center in Maryland, and currently maintains six district offices in Atlanta, Chicago, Dallas, Kansas City, New York, and San Francisco. In addition, the OCC has 72 field offices in cities throughout the United States, resident examiner teams in the 23 largest banking companies supervised, and an examining office in London, England.

The OCC is headed by the Comptroller of the Currency, who is appointed by the President, with the advice and consent of the Senate, for a five-year term. An executive committee comprised of the senior executives of the major operating units advises the Comptroller on policy and operational issues. The OCC's organizational structure is depicted in Figure 2.

Figure 2: OCC Organization Chart

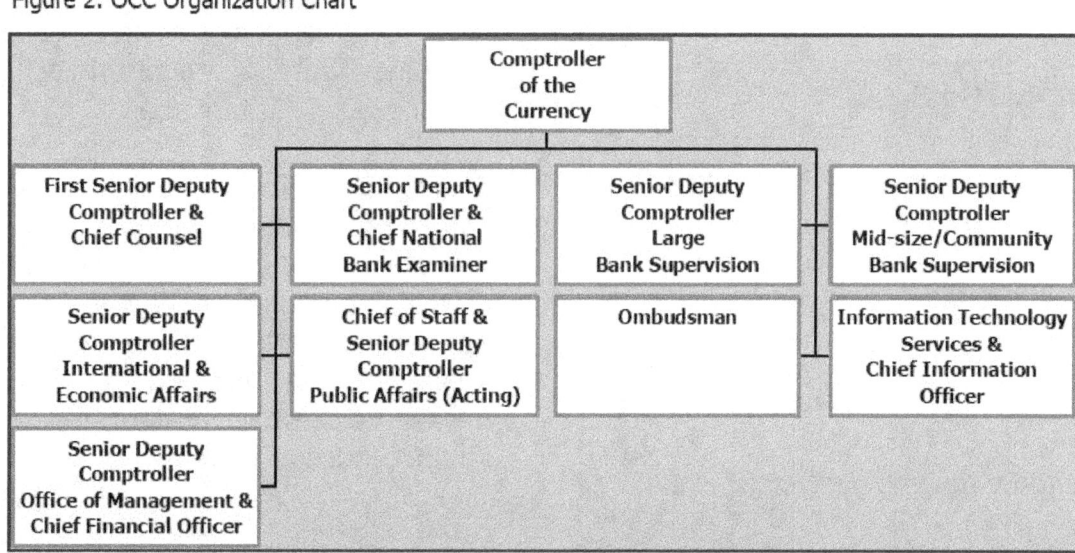

Part I – Management's Discussion and Analysis

MISSION AND VISION

Mission

The OCC charters, regulates, and supervises national banks to ensure a safe, sound, and competitive national banking system that supports the citizens, communities, and economy of the United States.

Vision

The OCC helps ensure that national banks soundly manage their risks, comply with applicable laws, compete effectively with other providers of financial services, offer products and services that meet the needs of customers, and provide fair access to financial services and fair treatment of their customers.

STRATEGIC GOALS AND PERFORMANCE MEASURES

Strategic Goals

The OCC supports the Department of the Treasury's strategic goals of:

- Promoting domestic economic growth,

- Improving customer satisfaction, and

- Improving employee satisfaction.

The OCC has established four strategic goals for achieving its mission. These goals are defined in the OCC's 2000–2005 Strategic Plan, as:

- A safe and sound national banking system,

- A flexible legal and regulatory framework that enables the national banking system to provide a full competitive array of financial services,

- Fair access to financial services and fair treatment of bank customers, and

- An expert, highly motivated and diverse workforce that makes effective use of OCC resources.

Performance Measures

As required by the Government Performance Results Act, the OCC issues an annual performance plan outlining the performance measures for the year. The OCC's performance measures help to demonstrate its progress in achieving its long-term strategic goals.

The OCC's performance data presented in this report is both reliable and complete. The performance data meets the OMB criteria that there is neither refusal nor marked reluctance by agency managers or government decision-makers to use the data in carrying out their responsibilities.

Part I – Management's Discussion and Analysis

Performance data is tracked using management information systems (MIS) that have sufficient systemic and management controls. The OCC managers certify that their systems of controls are adequate and operating effectively through the annual FMFIA process. The OCC's FMFIA process is discussed in more detail under Systems, Controls, and Legal Compliance beginning on page 44.

A complete list of the OCC's performance measures and the results achieved during FY 2002 are presented in Appendix A (page 81). The OCC's accomplishments on some key annual performance measures are incorporated in the Program Highlights beginning on page 8.

Part I – Management's Discussion and Analysis

PROGRAM HIGHLIGHTS

To achieve its strategic goals and accomplish its mission, the OCC aligns its activities into four major program areas: supervise, charter, regulate, and analyze risk. Three program areas are further divided into subprograms, as depicted in Figure 3.

The OCC's budget is formulated and expenditures are tracked by program area, as shown in Note 9 to the financial statements (page 79).

During FY 2002, the OCC faced significant challenges as a result of the nation's uncertain economy and the post-September 11 environment. The OCC's accomplishments amid these challenges are presented by program area.

Figure 3: OCC Programs and Subprograms

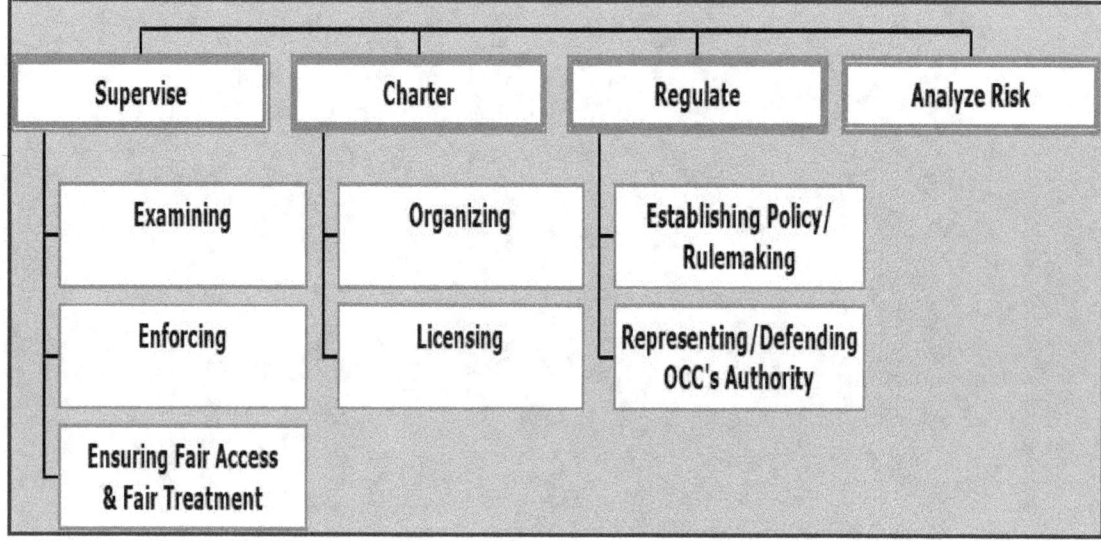

Part I – Management's Discussion and Analysis

Supervise Program

Figure 4: Supervise Subprograms

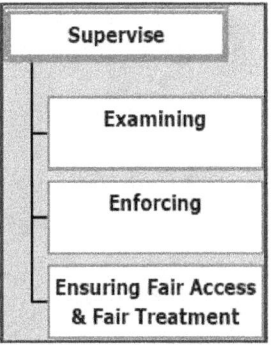

This program encompasses the on-going supervision of national banks or their subsidiaries, federal branches and agencies of foreign banks, national trust companies, bank data software vendors, and data processing service providers.

The OCC's Committee on Bank Supervision establishes and oversees areas of emphasis for the OCC's supervisory activities. The Committee is comprised of the Chief National Bank Examiner and the Senior Deputy Comptrollers for Large Bank Supervision and Mid-size/Community Bank Supervision.

The supervise program is by far the largest program and is the core for accomplishing the OCC's mission. For FY 2002, the OCC devoted 2,372 full-time equivalents[1] (FTEs) or 85 percent of total FTEs, to the supervise program. The cost of the supervise program was $360.4 million in FY 2002. The supervise program is further divided into three subprograms: examining,

enforcing, and ensuring fair access and fair treatment. The OCC's most significant supervision accomplishments are discussed by subprogram.

Examining

Examining activities include conducting regularly scheduled or targeted examinations and off-site analysis. During FY 2002, the OCC conducted over 3,100 bank examinations to ensure a strong national banking system that helps to sustain the U.S. economy. The distribution of the types of examinations conducted by the OCC is presented in Figure 5.

Figure 5: Type and Number of Bank Examinations

Type of Examination	Number of Exams
Safety and Soundness	1,508
Compliance	700
Community Reinvestment Act	384
Asset Management	313
Data Processing Servicers, Data Software Vendors, and Information Systems Operations	247

Examining also includes outreach meetings and presentations and appellate reviews for individual national banks through the ombudsman's office.

---

[1] Full-time equivalent is the number of paid hours accumulated during an entire fiscal year by a full-time position (40 hours per week). Generally, this is between 2,080 and 2,096 hours depending on the number of paid days that fall within a given fiscal year.

There are two business lines within this program, large banks and mid-size/community banks. The business line approach recognizes that institutions of varying sizes and complexity present different risks and require unique supervision philosophies.

The OCC's large bank program supervises the 23 largest national banking companies, using teams of dedicated on-site examiners. During FY 2002, areas of supervisory emphasis for the large bank program included credit underwriting, allowance for loan and lease loss reserve adequacy, operational and technology-related vulnerabilities, and internal controls.

Approximately 26 banking companies are in the OCC's mid-size bank program. During FY 2002, the OCC assigned dedicated examiners-in-charge for each of these companies and increased the resources devoted to their supervision.

The OCC's community bank program generally covers national banks with less than $1 billion in total assets. Banks are assigned to an OCC portfolio manager who oversees the supervisory strategies for the banks. These strategies combine on-site examinations and off-site analysis to monitor bank performance.

In community banks, the OCC also continued to refine its supervision-by-risk program that tailors examination strategies, resources, and activities to the risk profile of individual institutions. During FY 2002, the OCC implemented minimum core examination procedures for low-risk, stable community banks. These procedures establish the OCC's baseline level of testing and validation that are performed in every community bank. Expanded procedures are used in those institutions exhibiting higher risk.

Other activities in FY 2002 included anti-terrorist financing initiatives and special focused examinations.

Anti-Terrorist Financing Initiatives

The OCC completed a number of initiatives to respond to the USA PATRIOT Act requirements and the threat of terrorist financing in the national banking system. These initiatives included special reviews of selected banks to evaluate AML systems, including terrorist financing controls and USA PATRIOT Act compliance.

In addition, the OCC updated its AML training to include USA PATRIOT Act requirements and delivered the course to the OCC examiners and foreign bank supervisors. The OCC provided speakers for industry conferences on the subject of AML and the USA PATRIOT Act and participated in U.S. government anti-terrorist financing or AML initiatives involving other countries.

Part I – Management's Discussion and Analysis

Special Focused Examinations

Several focused supervisory activities were also conducted during FY 2002. The most significant of these activities were the examination of the OCC's credit card bank portfolio and the examination of national bank merchant processing activities.

The weak economy negatively affected the credit card industry during 2001 and 2002, particularly the subprime, mono-line credit card issuers that predominantly lend to high-risk consumers. Banks with high concentrations of these lines of business were a focus of the OCC's supervision activities in FY 2002. To systematically address the issues facing these banks, the OCC concurrently reviewed the operations of these banks and conducted additional training for the OCC's examiners and portfolio managers in various risk management, accounting, and capital issues associated with these activities.

The OCC also took additional steps to improve its supervision of merchant processing activities in mid-size and community banks. Banks with high-risk merchant processing businesses were identified, and examiners with specialized training in this subject were deployed to conduct examinations targeted at controlling this risk. These efforts resulted in the development and issuance of a comprehensive set of examination procedures for merchant processing activities.

National Bank Appeals

The national bank appeals process includes resolution of individual appeals and inquiries from national banks. With the consent of the Comptroller, the ombudsman has the discretion to stay any agency decision or action during the resolution of an appealable matter. During FY 2002, the ombudsman's office processed over 150 substantive actions including formal appeals and inquiries.

Enforcing

Enforcing ensures that the laws, regulations, and policies are followed by individual national banks. Activities include the OCC's formal enforcement actions, as well as more informal actions to support prompt detection and mitigation of problems before they affect a bank's viability.

During FY 2002, the OCC took various formal and informal enforcement actions, including entering into formal agreements and consent cease-and-desist orders with national banks engaging in violations of laws and regulations and/or unsafe or unsound banking practices; obtaining consent removal and/or prohibition orders; and ordering civil monetary penalties.

Part I – Management's Discussion and Analysis

Special Supervision

Special supervision involves activities related to managing problem banks. The OCC is implementing actions to strengthen the program for identifying and managing the current caseload of troubled institutions, facilitate earlier intervention in problem banks, and establish a mechanism for managing a potential increase in the caseload of problem banks. Actions completed during FY 2002, include:

- Restructuring the special supervision unit into a separate division with a deputy comptroller, effective November 2001, to bring more centralized oversight to problem banks;

- Training supervision management on the importance of prompt corrective action, the tools available to facilitate prompt corrective actions to issues identified during the supervisory process, and the importance of a sound supervision record to prevent failures and/or losses to the bank insurance fund;

- Requiring a rehabilitation/action plan on all 3-, 4-, and 5-rated institutions focusing on the long-term supervisory strategy for the bank, including assessments of the root causes of the problems, the viability of the bank's business plan, and the critical assumptions, or milestones for success; and

- Developing a new MIS focusing on predictors of future troubled banks, trends in the troubled institution population, and information needs focusing on individual troubled banks.

Ensuring Fair Access and Fair Treatment

Activities in this subprogram include: reviewing issues related to fair access to financial services and fair treatment of bank customers; educating community and consumer organizations and facilitating their interactions with the OCC; conducting outreach to national banks to assist them in meeting their obligations under the Community Reinvestment Act (CRA) rules; meeting with individuals and groups protesting banks' corporate applications; reviewing or approving individual bank community development activities; and conducting targeted fair lending examinations. The OCC's efforts to ensure fair access and fair treatment focused on fully integrating compliance risk supervision into the on-going supervision activities of national banks.

Part I – Management's Discussion and Analysis

Community Affairs

The OCC's community affairs staff conducted over 170 bank consultations during FY 2002. In addition, the OCC met with community and consumer organizations on policy matters related to predatory lending, payday lending, consumer protection, CRA changes, financial literacy, and other issues. These meetings provided the OCC information about the challenges and solutions to increased access to financial services for consumers in disadvantaged communities. Other activities are discussed under Partnership and Outreach (page 27).

Consumer Complaints

The OCC's Customer Assistance Group (CAG) reviews and processes complaints received from customers of national banks. The OCC maintains a call center with trained compliance professionals to deliver responsive customer service. The OCC's philosophy is to resolve cases on the first contact when possible. During FY 2002, the OCC received more than 80,000 calls and opened over 75,000 cases.

In addition, the OCC fully implemented CAGNet, a component of National BankNet. CAGNet, a web-based "business-to-business" application, was developed to help speed complaint resolution time and increase efficiency for both the banks and the CAG.

Through the CAGNet application, the consumer's complaint data is electronically delivered from the CAG to bank management for response. Likewise, bank management electronically submits a documented response to the CAG for review. Additionally, bank management has access to their current and historical complaint data through a standard set of reports. Currently, 30 banking companies are using this business-to-business application to respond to written customer complaints.

By facilitating communications between national banks and their customers, the CAG supports industry efforts to sustain a broad and satisfied customer base in a highly competitive financial services market. The group's constituents not only include customers of national banks, but also the national banks and the OCC's bank supervision divisions.

Performance Measures

The OCC established six performance measures for the supervise program and the results achieved are depicted in Figure 6.

Part I – Management's Discussion and Analysis

Figure 6: Target and Actual Performance of Supervise Performance Measures

Performance Measure	FY 2002	
	Target	Actual Performance
Percent of large and mid-size banks where quarterly risk assessments are completed	100%	100%
Percent of large and mid-size banks that received an annual report of examination	100%	97%
Percent of community bank examinations conducted in accordance with the FDICIA-mandated schedule, exclusive of approved exceptions	100%	98%
Percent of community bank examinations that are approved exceptions to the FDICIA-mandated schedule	≤ 10%	3%
Average calendar days past due on community bank examinations that do not meet the approved exception criteria	≤ 15	17
Average days to process customer complaints and consumer inquiries	50	44

The OCC achieved 97 percent of its target for reports of examination (ROE) issued to large and mid-size banks. An ROE is required for each individual charter so there can be multiple ROEs issued to any one banking company. An ROE for 152 of the 157 large and mid-

size bank charters was issued during the fiscal year. The OCC waived ROEs for the remaining five charters due to mergers that were in process or other overriding circumstances.

The OCC achieved 98 percent compliance with the FDICIA-mandated examination schedule for community banks. Mitigating circumstances prevent the OCC from achieving full compliance. For example, the prioritization of resources to higher risk institutions and scheduling anomalies preclude strict compliance with the FDICIA schedule.

The OCC limited approved exceptions to the FDICIA examination schedule to three percent, exceeding the target of no more than ten percent. Delays in examinations that did not meet the approved exception criteria averaged 17 days. The OCC's managers will continue to monitor and manage the initiation of examinations and limit the length of delays when resources are diverted to problem banks whenever possible.

In addition to the performance measures, the OCC exceeded its five customer service standards related to the examination of national banks (page 81). The customer service results were based on 874 examination questionnaires completed by banks during the year, which was a 49 percent response rate.

Part I – Management's Discussion and Analysis

Charter Program

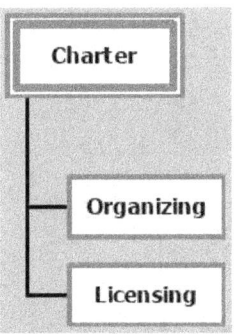

This program comprises the activities that result in the chartering of national banks and the evaluation of the permissibility of structures and activities of national banks and their subsidiaries. These activities include review and approval for new national bank charters, mergers, acquisitions, conversions, business combinations, corporate reorganizations, changes in control, operating subsidiaries, branches, relocations, and subordinated debt issues. The OCC devoted 79 FTEs to the charter program at a cost of $11.3 million during FY 2002.

The organizing subprogram includes the activities that relate to bringing new banks into the national banking system or approving new federal branches or agencies. During FY 2002, a total of 3,496 corporate applications were received by the OCC. The OCC made 1,554 decisions, 30 of these were for new national charters.

Electronic Filing of Licensing Applications

The OCC is developing e-Corp, a component of the National BankNet, to provide banks the ability to file applications electronically. Initially, electronic filing will be limited to branch and relocation applications.

In FY 2002, development efforts focused on ensuring that the branch and relocation applications are in compliance with Section 508 of the Rehabilitation Act of 1973, as amended (29 USC 794(d)), giving disabled employees and members of the public access to information that is comparable to the access available to others.

Developmental efforts also focused on implementing an electronic signature for e-Corp applications. At year-end, branch and relocation applications had been tested internally and bank testing had begun.

Performance Measures

The OCC exceeded its target by processing 96 percent of corporate applications in accordance with its published timeframes. The OCC also exceeded its five customer service standards for providing timely and quality licensing services (page 82). These results were based on 594 licensing surveys received from applicants during the year, which was a 52 percent response rate.

Part I – Management's Discussion and Analysis

Regulate Program

Figure 8: Regulate Subprograms

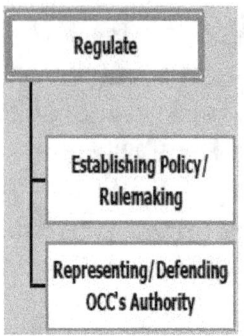

This program comprises the activities that establish regulations, policies, and procedures that apply to all national banks and the supervision of those banks or activities that defend the OCC's supervisory authority over the national banking system.

The OCC devoted 173 FTEs at a total cost of $25 million to the regulate program during FY 2002. The establishing policy/rulemaking subprogram includes activities to establish or interpret national banking regulations, policies, procedures, and operating guidance. The representing/defending the OCC's authority subprogram includes activities that develop the OCC's positions or defend national bank powers through interpretation or litigation.

Regulations

The OCC issued 12 final rules in FY 2002. Rulemaking efforts included USA PATRIOT Act implementation, capital issues, and codifications of permissible electronic banking activities. Significant rules included:

- *Capital Treatment of Recourse Arrangements and Direct Credit Substitutes.* 66 Fed. Reg. 59614 (November 29, 2001).

- *Capital Treatment of Nonfinancial Equity Investments.* 67 Fed. Reg. 3784 (January 25, 2002).

- *Electronic Activities.* 67 Fed. Reg. 34992 (May 17, 2002).

- *International Banking Activities: Capital Equivalency Deposit.* 67 Fed. Reg. 41619 (June 19, 2002).

- *Customer Identification Program.* 67 Fed. Reg. 48290 (July 23, 2002).

Interpretations and Opinions

The OCC issued several significant legal opinions during FY 2002 pertaining to the applicability of state law to national banks in the areas of insurance and national bank operating subsidiaries. Several legal opinions addressed specific circumstances in the securities area. The OCC continues to publish information on significant interpretations and actions on its Web site.

The OCC also issued guidance on the ability of national banks to hedge risks arising from bank-permissible, equity derivative transactions; the fiduciary activities of national banks; and small-bank compliance with the privacy regulations mandated by the Gramm-Leach-Bliley Act (GLBA).

Part I – Management's Discussion and Analysis

In support of the OCC's operations, legal interpretations and advice were issued in the following areas: community bank lending limits for an OCC pilot program, inappropriate use of the national bank charter in certain payday lending arrangements, predatory lending issues in general, and structured early intervention and resolutions of problem banks.

Policies and Procedures

The OCC issued policies and procedures during FY 2002 to address a variety of supervisory and licensing issues. The *Comptroller's Handbook* series was updated with new booklets providing expanded examination procedures in the areas of personal fiduciary services, custody services, insurance activities, and merchant processing.

Supervisory bulletins were issued to bankers and examiners on various risk and risk management issues, including: unsafe and unsound investment portfolio practices, the use and management of third-party service providers and vendors, credit risk arising from certain investment portfolio safekeeping arrangements, and the risks associated with automated clearing house transactions conducted through the Internet.

As noted in the Partnership and Outreach section on page 27, the OCC in conjunction with the other federal financial regulators also issued guidance on technical capital, accounting, operational, and supervisory issues associated with the sale and securitization of bank assets; country risk management; and the risks and supervisory treatment of parallel-owned banking organizations.

With regard to licensing and chartering activities, the *Comptroller's Licensing Manual* was reconfigured in a primarily electronic format, enabling the OCC to make regular updates more efficiently. The OCC also prepared to re-issue guidance on tribal ownership of national banks, developed policy for expedited corporate reorganizations, and developed policy on extended safeguards in the form of conditions and agreements to address safety and soundness concerns in licensing application approvals.

Representation of the OCC in Court

The OCC is a party in court cases, or files as *amicus,* to protect national banks' exercise of their powers (e.g., to sell insurance or to charge reasonable fees for their services), and to protect the authority of the OCC to enforce applicable state laws against national banks.

Litigation includes defending the OCC's regulations from judicial challenges and the OCC's enforcement actions and decisions to place banks into receivership. Notable court cases in FY 2002 include several matters related to preemption of state law by federal law.

Part I – Management's Discussion and Analysis

Analyze Risk Program

This program consists of activities to identify, analyze, and respond to emerging systemic risks and trends that could affect an individual national bank or the entire national banking system. During FY 2002, the OCC devoted 168 FTEs at a total cost of $25.7 million to the analyze risk program.

The program's key objectives are the early identification of higher-risk institutions, activities, and trends and potential shocks to the system. Areas of analysis include: bank lending and credit risk; economics, finance, and core banking; industry studies; international bank supervision and regulations; emerging risks; evolving business practices and financial market issues; capital markets activities; and asset securitization.

Under this program, analytical tools and models were developed to assist supervision in tailoring examination procedures based on risk profiles and allocating resources accordingly. The OCC has developed two tools that enhance the identification of and supervisory responses to emerging risks; one is focused on community banks and one is focused on large banks.

Community Bank Canary

The "Community Bank Canary" tool provides a menu of financial risk measures and benchmarks, predictive models, market barometers, and research tools that are used to identify community banks with potentially high or complex amounts of financial risk, as well as banks that have low and stable financial risk.

During FY 2002, the financial risk measures were enhanced by incorporating rates of change in a bank's risk profile. This enhancement allows examiners to monitor current risk levels and trends in risk levels for a bank or group of banks.

Large Bank Canary

The OCC implemented the "Large Bank Canary" tool in FY 2002. It captures static benchmarks for five financial risks (credit, interest rate, liquidity, price, and foreign currency), strategic risk, asset management activities, and securitization activities. A separate historical data page contains balance sheet and income statement figures and ratios. Summary Canary reports were created, and include a cover page with summary information from markets, models, and internal sources for all large banks along with a financial snapshot with summary balance sheet and income statement items for each large bank.

The OCC has several additional tools and models that assist in the identification and analysis of systemic risks, including a "Credit Risk Analytics" tool that combines bank portfolio data with a number of pre-established risk metrics to provide exposure size, quality, and rate-of-change information for 52 standard industry groupings. During FY 2002, the number of exposures captured was expanded to approximately 60 percent of commercial credit exposures in the national banking system.

Part I – Management's Discussion and Analysis

Management of the OCC

In accomplishing its mission, the OCC is committed to the effective, efficient, and economical management of its resources. Some of the OCC's management initiatives during FY 2002, including the President's Management Agenda (PMA), are discussed below.

President's Management Agenda

The basic tenets underlying the OCC's fourth strategic goal embody many of the same issues included in the PMA. During FY 2002, the OCC developed plans to achieve the goals of each PMA initiative. A brief discussion of the OCC's PMA accomplishments follows.

Budget and Performance Integration

In FY 2002, the OCC developed strategic, outcome-oriented performance measures to better demonstrate the effect of the OCC's regulatory activities on the national banking system. The new performance measures are linked to the OCC's strategic goals and program areas, and are included in the FY 2003 Annual Performance Plan.

The OCC also implemented an integrated planning, budgeting, and evaluation process for the development of the FY 2003 budget and performance plan. The results of program reviews and execution of the FY 2002 budget were used in the budget deliberations for FY 2003. Additionally, organizational operating plans identified planned activities and anticipated performance to support the budget requests.

The OCC began an initiative to develop staffing models to better substantiate budget requests and to modify the project/activity structure for tracking labor hours. These efforts will lay the foundation to capture useful cost accounting and unit cost information for more informed decision-making in the future.

Competitive Sourcing

The OMB established a FY 2002 goal requiring agencies to cost compare or commercially compete five percent of the FTE positions listed on their Calendar Year (CY) 2000 Federal Activities Inventory Reform Act inventory. For the OCC's inventory, the five percent equated to 14 positions for cost comparison. During FY 2002, the OCC cost compared a total of 20 positions, exceeding the goal established by OMB. All 20 positions were retained in-house because it was more cost effective than obtaining these services commercially.

Expanded E-Government

As a result of working with the Department of the Treasury and OMB this year, the OCC's business cases for its FY 2003 information technology investments improved and better met the intent of the OMB's guidance and the goals of the PMA.

The OCC's Investment Review Board reviewed the FY 2003 proposed technology projects and recommended investment decisions to the executive committee and the Comptroller.

The OCC is within 95 percent of planned cost, schedule, and performance targets for its FY 2002 technology investments. The OCC also will evaluate completed projects one year after implementation to ensure that the system is meeting the needs of the users and supporting its mission, using appropriate technology.

The OCC is in the preliminary stage of data gathering for its technical and business architectures, as well as the Technical Reference Model. A Framework and Enterprise Architecture (EA) Roadmap that support the Department of the Treasury and Federal EA Framework have been developed. It is being reviewed for alignment with the OCC's strategic plan and the potential targeted architecture.

Improving Financial Management

On October 1, 2001, the OCC implemented a JFMIP certified financial and acquisitions management system that provides timely and accurate financial data to manage operations. This system is discussed in more detail under the Financial Management Discussion beginning on page 35. Additionally, the OCC closed its

accounting records for month-end financial reporting in both a timely and accurate manner.

Human Capital

In December 2001, the OCC began to implement its Strategic Plan for Active Recruitment, Retention, and Career Development, which outlines the OCC's five-year plan for achieving its strategic human capital objectives.

In FY 2002, all managers and employees had performance plans that included performance accountability measures linked to achievement of the OCC's strategic priorities. The OCC's performance management program is used in concert with a performance based compensation program.

The OCC has defined mission-critical competencies and identified skill gaps. The OCC established the Examiner Specialized Skills program to ensure a sufficient pipeline of qualified candidates for positions in the following areas of expertise: bank technology, capital markets, retail credit risk, asset management, and compliance. In addition, training plans were implemented to increase expertise in asset management, bank information technology, and capital markets. To ensure the OCC is adequately prepared for the future, a management succession planning process was approved and management succession plans for all functional areas will be developed.

The OCC expanded its work-life programs by offering a maxi flex alternative in addition to the compressed work schedule program and broader opportunities for work-at-home. The OCC also expanded its Alternative Dispute Resolution program to maximize dispute prevention strategies and potentially avert EEO complaints.

Real Estate Strategic Study

To realign the OCC's real estate portfolio in direct support of its mission, a real estate strategic study was completed. Recommendations to positively affect operational, fiscal, technological, personnel, and program goals were implemented. The OCC has realized savings of approximately $1.8 million on leases negotiated during FY 2002.

District Restructuring Study

During FY 2002, the OCC completed an internal study to examine the various functions and services provided by its district offices. The purpose of this study was to evaluate whether the locations from which, and the means by which, district office functions are being performed are optimal and best aligned with the OCC's long-term supervisory strategy. The results indicated that change is needed to ensure the district office operations are appropriately aligned for the future.

The geographical footprint and size of the district offices have remained essentially unchanged since 1983, when the OCC reduced from 12 regional offices to six district offices. Since then, there has been significant consolidation within the banking industry, as well as material changes in the nature and functions of the OCC's district offices. The cumulative effect of these trends over the past 20 years changes the distribution needs of the OCC's district resources.

Consequently, the OCC decided to restructure the current six district offices into four locations. By January 2004, the OCC will combine the San Francisco and Kansas City district offices into a new district office in Denver, and will consolidate the Atlanta and Dallas offices in Dallas. The OCC will retain field offices in San Francisco, Kansas City, and Atlanta.

Learning Management System

The OCC selected a software package and began implementation of a Learning Management System (LMS). The LMS will allow the OCC to deliver a portion of its internal training curricula to employees through an on-line "E-learning." E-learning is one alternative delivery method that can be more effective, less costly, and less disruptive for training the workforce, especially one like the OCC's that is geographically dispersed. E-learning is considered an industry best practice. The LMS also updates and replaces the OCC's obsolete Training Administration System.

Windows 2000 Upgrade

The OCC modernized personal computer software for all employees, overhauled the Microsoft network infrastructure nation-wide to support future applications, and revamped remote access services with a single sign-on solution.

Information Technology Infrastructure Upgrades

The OCC completed a major upgrade to the data center electrical system. The new equipment improves power reliability and provides additional electrical capacity for future growth. The OCC also upgraded 22 data circuits to full T-1 speeds to improve network performance for large offices that were experiencing congestion on the slower lines.

Part I – Management's Discussion and Analysis

Program Evaluations

The OCC has several programs designed to evaluate the effectiveness and efficiency of programs and operations. The results of internal program reviews are used to improve the management of the OCC. During FY 2002, numerous internal reviews were conducted.

Program Analysis Unit Reviews

The Program Analysis unit (PAU) conducted reviews supporting the Comptroller's expectation for a credible and effective resource management process. The PAU completed an information technology infrastructure study, evaluated the London Office, prepared an analysis of alternative work locations, completed an evaluation of supervision operations, evaluated resource requests made by the Information Technology office and the CAG, and completed various analysis of policy, programs, budgetary, and management issues related to the OCC's programs.

Supervision Quality Reviews

Quality assurance reviews conducted in FY 2002 were used to provide internal feedback on the effectiveness of the OCC's bank supervision activities. These reviews covered community bank supervision; federal branch and agency supervision; problem bank lessons-learned; Financial Institutions Reform, Recovery and Enforcement Act Section 914; and follow-up reviews.

Licensing Quality Reviews

Several aspects of the OCC's licensing activities were reviewed during FY 2002. The OCC conducted quality reviews of licensing in two districts with the highest volume of charters to determine adherence to policies and procedures. The OCC also reviewed chartering processes through a charter renovation project. As a result, the OCC identified best practices, implemented enhancements to the charter process, and improved written policies and procedures.

Part I – Management's Discussion and Analysis

Management Challenges and High-Risk Areas

The OCC believes a major challenge and risk to maintaining a strong banking industry is ensuring adequate and equitable funding for bank supervision. The OCC will continue its efforts to bring attention and focus to this issue. The current funding arrangement, under which state banks are subsidized by their federal supervisors, is unfair to national banks, which are forced to contribute to the subsidization of their state-chartered competitors while bearing the full cost of their own supervision. It also disrupts the constructive competition between state and federal bank regulators that is a cornerstone of the dual banking system. Additionally, it compromises the safety and soundness of all U.S. banks.

National banks pay the full costs of their supervision through assessments to the OCC. Conversely, state banks pay only the portion of their supervision costs that is provided by state supervisory agencies. In 2001, for example, national banks paid 100 percent of their supervision costs while state banks paid just 22 percent of their supervision costs.

This inequity is compounded because the FDIC uses a substantial portion of the income generated from national banks' accumulated deposit insurance premiums to supervise state nonmember banks. The Federal Reserve System's supervision costs are borne by all taxpayers because operating expenses are subtracted from earnings on government securities before paying the remainder to the U.S. Treasury for the benefit of taxpayers. Historically, the choice between a national or state charter centered on such things as supervisory philosophy and responsiveness, examination quality, and the scope of permissible activities. Today, the cost of supervision has become an increasingly more important factor in a bank's choice of charter, rather than those factors that enhance the overall quality of bank supervision.

The most serious concern is that the current funding system works to reduce supervisory resources when they are most likely to be needed. During times of widespread stress in the banking system, healthy national banks are asked to pay higher assessments so that the OCC can deal with a rising number of problem banks. As a result, the financial incentive for healthy national banks to convert to a state charter increases, depleting the revenue needed to protect safety and soundness.

Inspector General

In 2002, the Treasury's Office of the Inspector General (OIG) did not cite any management challenges or high-risk areas specific to the OCC. The Inspector General's memorandum to the Secretary of the Treasury cited five overarching challenges for the Department. The OCC has focused on four of these challenges at the bureau level. Two challenges, Linking Resources to Results and Financial Management Systems, were previously discussed under the PMA on page 20 and are elaborated on in the Financial Management Discussion on page 35. The third challenge, information security, is discussed in the Government Information Security Reform Act of 2000 (GISRA) section on page 45.

The fourth challenge is prompt corrective action to audit findings. In FY 2002, the OCC developed a quarterly report on the status of open corrective actions to audit recommendations. The purpose of the report is to bring more executive-level attention and involvement in establishing realistic completion dates for planned corrective actions and the timely implementation of those actions.

The fifth challenge identified by the OIG related to duplicate, wasteful practices for similar activities performed across bureaus is more appropriately addressed at the Department level.

Part I – Management's Discussion and Analysis

Partnership and Outreach

The OCC works with other regulators, industry, and community and consumer organizations to further the OCC's mission and to accomplish its strategic goals and objectives in an effective and efficient manner.

Federal Financial Regulators

Primarily through the Federal Financial Institutions Examination Council (FFIEC), the OCC works closely with the other federal financial regulators (Board of Governors of the Federal Reserve System, FDIC, Office of Thrift Supervision, and National Credit Union Administration) to coordinate supervisory policies, regulations and regulatory reporting requirements, and examiner training on issues that cut across the banking system. These efforts reduce regulatory burden by promoting greater uniformity, consistency, and efficiency in the supervision of insured depository institutions.

During FY 2002, the FFIEC regulators completed numerous initiatives to address emerging risks and issues facing the industry, including:

- Amendments to their risk-based capital guidelines to better align the level of capital that banks must hold with the risks that they undertake. The changes addressed recourse, direct credit substitutes, and residual interests in asset securitizations;

merchant banking activities; and claims on securities firms.

- Supervisory guidance to bankers on risks posed by bank activities, methods banks can use to manage those risks, and factors examiners will use to evaluate the adequacy of a bank's risk management practices. Interagency guidance was issued on:

  1) Technical capital, accounting, operational, and supervisory issues associated with the sale and securitization of bank assets;

  2) Risk management principles for economic, social, and political conditions and events in a foreign country that may affect a U.S. bank's financial condition; and

  3) The characteristics of, and potential risks associated with, certain types of bank organization structures, known as parallel-owned banking organizations, that arise when a U.S. depository institution and foreign bank are controlled directly or indirectly by the same person or group of persons.

- Implementing regulations for the USA PATRIOT Act.

- Updated communications protocols for emergency situations in response to the events of September 11th.

- On-going joint, supervisory programs such as the shared examination programs, including the Shared National Credit (SNC) program, the Interagency Country Exposure Review Committee, and the interagency examination program for multi-regional data processing servicers. Through the 2002 SNC program, examiners collectively reviewed approximately 10,000 credit facilities representing over $1.9 trillion in credit exposures.

Other Domestic and International Regulators

The OCC also works with other state, federal, and international regulators and supervisors on matters of mutual interest.

Consistent with the GLBA, the OCC has entered into information-sharing agreements with 37 state insurance departments and meets regularly with the National Association of Insurance Commissioners.

The OCC works closely with the Securities and Exchange Commission on various securities, brokerage, and accounting and disclosure issues and with the Federal Trade Commission on various consumer protection and privacy issues.

The OCC is a member of the Administration's Financial and Banking Infrastructure Information Committee and is working actively with the Department of the Treasury to implement the President's anti-terrorist initiatives.

On the international front, the OCC is actively involved in the Basel Committee on Banking Supervision's efforts to update and revise the Basel Capital Accord to make the capital standards required of internationally active banks more comprehensive, risk sensitive, and reflective of advances in banks' risk measurement and management practices.

The Comptroller chairs the Basel Committee's Electronic Bank Working Group.

Industry and Community Outreach

The OCC maintains an active dialog with key constituents that are affected by and interested in the OCC's mission. The Comptroller and senior management seek input and feedback on issues facing the banking industry through outreach meetings with industry and trade associations. During FY 2002, the OCC participated in or conducted 217 outreach activities. Highlights of these activities include:

- Co-sponsoring the Hispanic Banking Forum and the National Community and Economic Development Conference to share success stories and strategies for expanding financial access to underserved markets and populations.

- Conducting outreach meetings targeted for the mid-size bank portfolio, including a Chief Executive Officer Roundtable, a Chief Credit Officer Forum, and a Retail Credit Forum.

- Conducting telephone seminars for bankers. These seminars allowed bankers to listen to agency experts discuss their experiences and policy imperatives and interact with them during a question-and-answer session. The topics were: (1) Audit Roundtable on Risk Assessment and Internal Controls, (2) Audit Roundtable on Work Papers and Audit Committee Reporting, (3) Outsourcing Your Audit Function, and (4) Risk Management Principles for Third-Party Relationships.

- Conducting workshops on *Understanding OCC's Risk Assessment Process*, for approximately 350 community bank directors. The goal was to enhance their understanding of risk-based supervision; increase familiarity with major risks in commercial banking; learn the types of questions to ask managers, auditors, and examiners; and review common ways to identify, measure, monitor, and control risk.

- Providing bankers access to Comparative Analysis Reporting that has selected financial data/ratios for over 8,700 institutions, including all commercial banks and FDIC-insured savings banks. National banks use this information to analyze and compare their performance with peer banks or other banks in the same city, county, or state. Additionally this information may be used when a bank is considering acquiring or merging with another bank.

OCC's Next Steps

The OCC will continue to monitor and evaluate risks to individual national banks and the national banking system and incorporate the results of these risk analyses into its supervision strategies. Key issues to be addressed by the OCC's supervision activities include: credit quality; adequacy of allowance for loan and lease losses; scrutiny of accounting practices; integrity of management information systems; off-balance sheet activities; funding issues; preparation for implementation of the revised Basel Capital Accord; and risks associated with managing third-party service providers.

Bank Secrecy Act/anti-money-laundering issues in the post-September 11th environment, security of customer information, and business continuity also will be prominent supervision issues. Early resolution of problem bank situations will be pursued to minimize losses to the bank insurance fund and interagency collaboration and coordination remain important in resolving critical issues impacting the banking industry.

In addition, the OCC will enhance and improve its technology solutions for responding to and dealing with the public and the population of national banks in the most efficient manner. The OCC will activate e-Corp for the filing of branch and relocations applications in CY 2003. The OCC also will develop electronic filing capabilities for other types of corporate applications. In addition, the OCC will initiate efforts to more effectively use the data from the e-Corp applications to develop a pilot or proof of concept repository for critical application and institution information.

PART II

FINANCIAL DISCUSSION AND ANALYSIS

Letter from the Chief Financial Officer

I am pleased to present the OCC's financial statements as an integral part of the "Performance and Accountability Report" for FY 2002. For FY 2002, our independent auditors rendered an unqualified opinion with no material weaknesses.

Consistent with the PMA, the OCC continues to make great strides in improving financial management and budget and performance integration. Highlights of some of our significant accomplishments during the past year, include:

- The OCC received a "green" rating under the PMA from the Department of the Treasury for financial management by providing accurate and timely interim financial information; having financial management systems that meet federal requirements; having appropriate controls over erroneous payments; and receiving an unqualified and timely audit opinion on our annual financial statements.

- The OCC successfully implemented an integrated, JFMIP certified, financial and acquisitions management system (called "$MART"). Many of our business processes related to processing financial transactions, from procurement through disbursement, were re-engineered. As a result, the Comptroller issued a certification of reasonable assurance for FMFIA Section 4 and substantial compliance with FFMIA.

- The OCC integrated its planning, budgeting, and program evaluation processes. Significant improvements were made to our performance measures to better capture the effect of our activities on the national banking system. Our deliberative process in finalizing the FY 2003 budget and performance plan was a more informed process using the results of program reviews, data on actual expenditures, and operating plans. These efforts, combined with the capabilities provided by the $MART system, move the OCC forward in the integration of budget and performance.

- During FY 2002, the OCC made advancements in the implementation of its reserve policy whereby funds are earmarked for rare events that could disrupt on-going operations. By fiscal year-end, the reserved funds had reached 86 percent of the targeted reserve level of $225 million to help ensure the OCC's mission is accomplished.

- The OCC implemented corrective actions to address two reportable conditions from last year's audit. These reportable conditions have been downgraded to management letter comments in the current fiscal year's report.

I am proud that the OCC now has a record of accurate and reliable financial reporting, and I am particularly proud of the important improvements we made to financial management during the past fiscal year. Our goals for FY 2003 and beyond include upgrading our $MART system, implementing a new travel and time entry system, and continuing our progress on the PMA initiatives.

This report has been posted to our Web site at http://www.occ.treas.gov.

Edward J. Hanley
November 15, 2002

FINANCIAL MANAGEMENT DISCUSSION

Major Accomplishments

During FY 2002, the OCC's financial management initiatives focused on improving financial accountability, enhancing financial systems, re-engineering the planning, budgeting and program evaluation process, strengthening internal controls over time entry and travel programs, and documenting financial policies and procedures. A more detailed discussion of these initiatives follows.

Financial Accountability

The OCC continues to give a high priority to providing accurate and reliable financial data to its customers. Towards that end, the OCC met the Secretary of the Treasury's challenge of achieving a 3-day close for producing the OCC's monthly and quarterly financial statements for FY 2002, receiving a "green" rating for data quality. The OCC met the Secretary's accelerated schedule for preparing audited financial statements for FY 2002. By meeting this deadline the OCC, along with other Treasury bureaus, will enable the Department to prepare its audited financial statements by the OMB's November 15 deadline, two years before the mandate takes place.

The OCC received an unqualified opinion on its FY 2002 financial statements with no material weaknesses. Throughout the fiscal year, the OCC focused on correcting all prior year audit and financial management issues, thereby strengthening the integrity of its financial data and operations. As a result, two reportable conditions from the previous fiscal year were downgraded to management letter comments and all other issues were resolved.

Financial Systems

On October 1, 2001, the OCC implemented $MART, its new Management and Accountability Reporting Tools system. This fully integrated system, which complies with federal financial management system requirements, provides the OCC's executives with real-time financial information on demand with a variety of reporting and query tools that foster successful program management.

During FY 2002, the OCC proceeded with a number of initiatives to improve the functionality of the system. The OCC tested an upgrade of the system's software to be implemented in FY 2003, expanded the system's reporting capabilities, and refined the design and controls for all automated interfaces.

Part II – Financial Discussion and Analysis

The OCC also implemented a new Asset Management module to improve the process for tracking accountable property.

Over the next two fiscal years, the OCC plans to move to an intranet-based platform for its core financial functions, implement new time entry and travel management systems, and develop a method to improve program costing.

Planning, Budgeting, and Program Evaluation Process

As discussed under the PMA (page 20), the OCC has made great strides in re-engineering its planning, budgeting, and program evaluation processes into an integrated program. This new process was designed to:

- Set strategic goals, objectives, and annual performance plans and link them to the budget through a program and project structure to promote programmatic, organizational, and budget object-class formulation;

- Measure performance and link performance measurement with the budget;

- Improve the internal management of the OCC's human and capital resources by providing more objective information for decision-making; and

- Improve the budget formulation process through the enhancement of analytic review of budget submissions.

Time Entry and Travel Program

In recognizing the need to improve controls over its time entry and travel reporting systems, the OCC implemented two nation-wide audit programs focused on the random selection and evaluation of time entry documents and travel vouchers. In a separate audit program of sensitive payments, the OCC conducted a 100 percent review of travel vouchers for all senior executives on a bi-weekly basis. The OCC also enhanced its controls over infrequent traveler accounts and strengthened its oversight of both individually- and centrally-billed charge card accounts. These efforts helped to minimize unauthorized purchases, delinquent accounts, and erroneous payments.

Policies and Procedures

The OCC completed its documentation of financial policies and procedures for a variety of processes, including sensitive payments, debt collection, assessment fee waivers, and revenue recognition and updated the *Comptroller's Handbook for Travel*.

Part II – Financial Discussion and Analysis

Funding Sources

The OCC does not receive congressional appropriations. Operations are primarily funded by assessments collected from national banks and income on investments in U.S. Treasury Securities. Figures 9 and 10 depict the sources of the OCC's funding for FYs 2002 and 2001.

Figure 9: FY 2002 Funding Sources

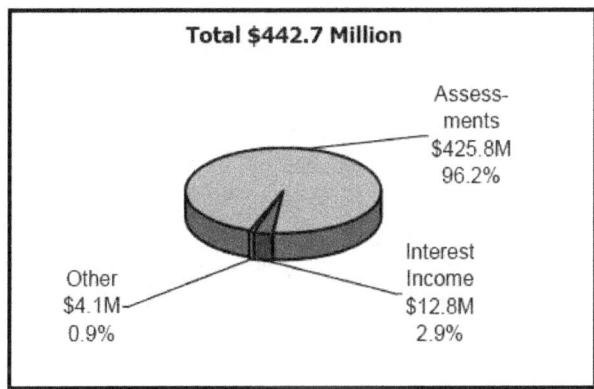

Figure 10: FY 2001 Funding Sources

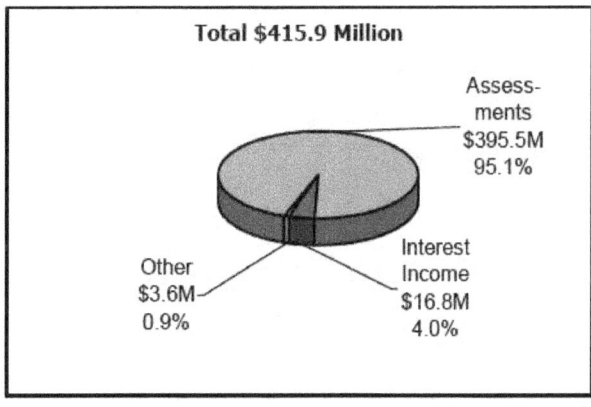

The OCC's funding sources increased by nearly $26.8 million principally resulting from a rise in assessments collected in FY 2002. National bank asset growth and the movement of assets into the national banking system were the impetus for higher assessments received in FY 2002.

Figures 11 and 12 show the composition of national bank assets and assessments collected from large banks, mid-size banks, community banks, and federal branches for FY 2002.

Figure 11: FY 2002 Composition of National Bank Assets

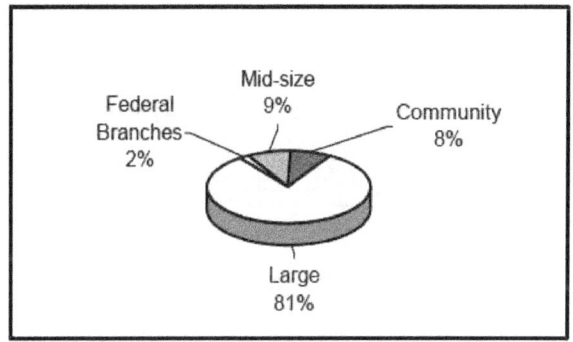

Figure 12: FY 2002 Assessment Revenue by Bank

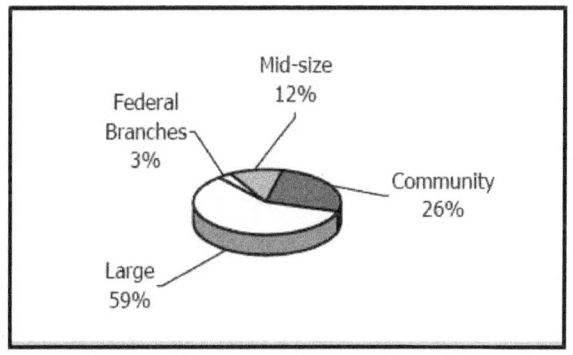

Part II – Financial Discussion and Analysis

Funding Uses

In FY 2002, the OCC's total expenses were $422.4 million, an increase of .5 percent over their level in FY 2001. The OCC's operations are personnel-intensive. In FY 2002, personnel compensation and benefits, travel, education and relocation expenses were $336.9 million or 79.8 percent of total expenses as compared to $325.5 or 77.5 percent of total expenses in FY 2001. In addition, the OCC experienced a $9.1 million or 9.6 percent decrease in non-personnel related expenses.

Figures 13 and 14 depict the uses of the OCC's funding for FYs 2002 and 2001.

Figure 13: FY 2002 Funding Uses

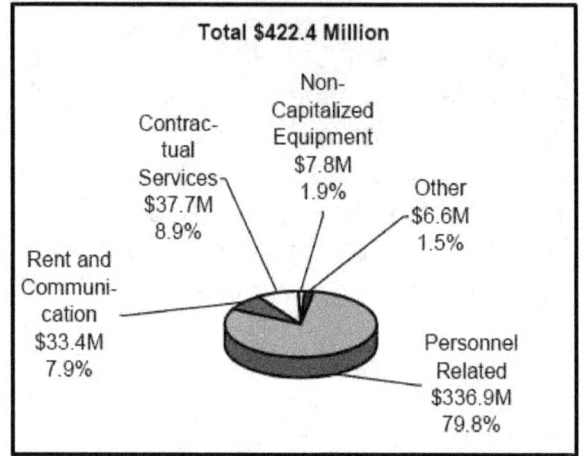

Figure 14: FY 2001 Funding Uses

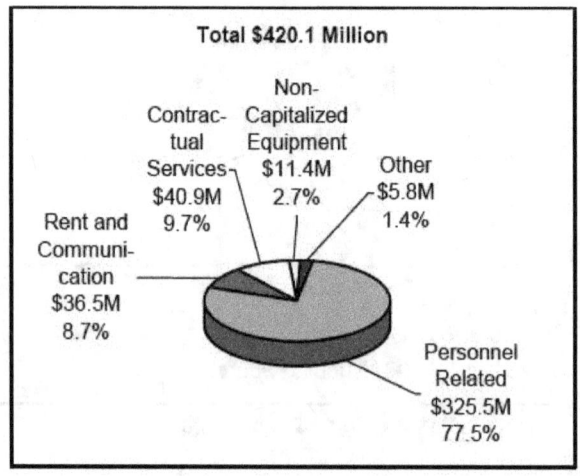

Part II – Financial Discussion and Analysis

Financial Review

The OCC received an unqualified opinion on its FY 2002 and 2001 financial statements. The financial statements include a *Balance Sheet and Statements of Net Cost, Changes in Net Position, Budgetary Resources, and Financing.* The financial statements and notes are presented on a comparative basis providing financial information for FYs 2002 and 2001. These financial statements summarize the OCC's financial activity and position. Highlights of information presented on the financial statements are provided below.[2]

Balance Sheet

The *Balance Sheet*, as of September 30, 2002 and 2001, presents the amounts that are owned by the OCC and available for use (assets), the amounts due to others or held for future recognition (liabilities), and the amounts that comprise the residual (net position). For clarity in presentation, assets and liabilities are differentiated between those resulting from transactions between the OCC and other federal entities (intragovernmental) and transactions between the OCC and non-federal entities.

Composition of and Trends in OCC Assets

The *Balance Sheet* shows that total assets as of September 30, 2002, increased by $45.2 million from their level at September 30, 2001. The increase of $38.0 million in *Investments and Related Interest* was due to a rise in assessment collections during FY 2002. The increase of $6.2 million in *Property and Equipment* was due primarily to software purchases. The composition of the OCC's assets is shown in Figures 15 and 16.

Figure 15: Composition of FY 2002 Assets

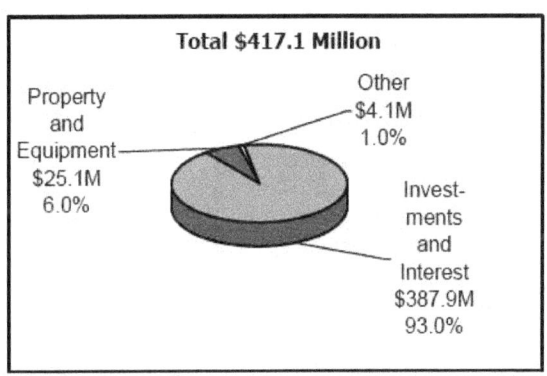

Figure 16: Composition of FY 2001 Assets

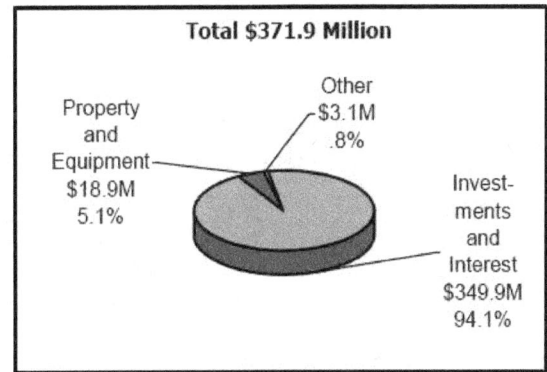

---

[2] All figures are rounded to the highest number or percent.

Part II – Financial Discussion and Analysis

Composition of and Trends in OCC Liabilities

Total liabilities as of September 30, 2002, increased by a net of $7.3 million over their level at September 30, 2001. The increase of $9.5 million in *Deferred Revenue* was due to a rise in assessment collections during FY 2002. The decrease of $2.8 million in *Accounts Payable and Accruals* was due to a variance in the accrual period between FYs 2002 and 2001. The composition of the OCC's liabilities is shown in Figures 17 and 18.

Composition of and Trends in OCC Net Position

The OCC's Net Position at $251.7 million as of September 30, 2002, and $213.8 million as of September 30, 2001, represents the cumulative net excess of the OCC's revenues over its cost of operations. The OCC reserves the majority of Net Position to supplement resources made available to fund the OCC's annual budget and to cover unforeseeable events. The composition of the OCC's net position is shown in Figures 19 and 20.

Figure 17: Composition of FY 2002 Liabilities

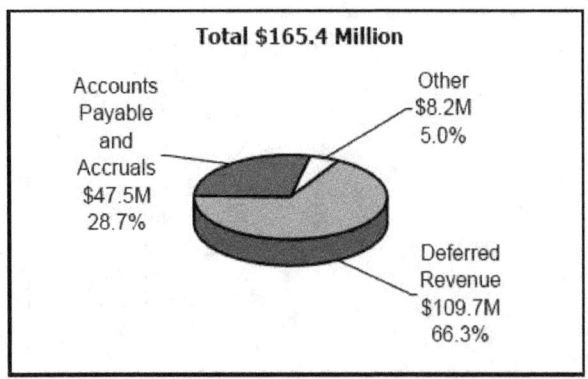

Figure 19: Composition of FY 2002 Net Position

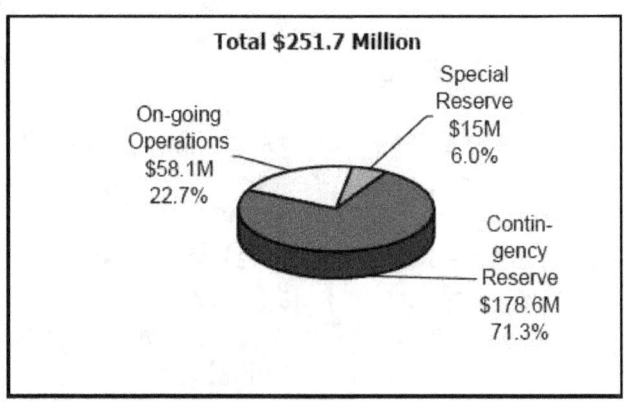

Figure 18: Composition of FY 2001 Liabilities

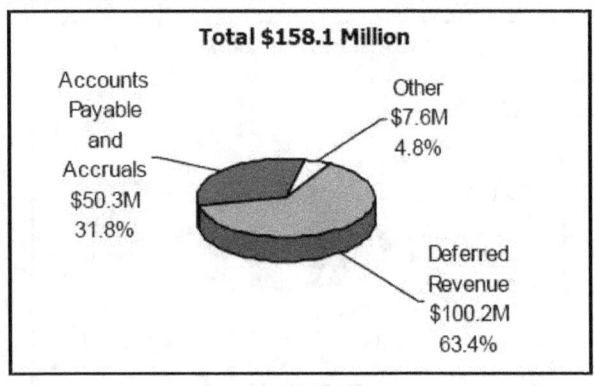

Figure 20: Composition of FY 2001 Net Position

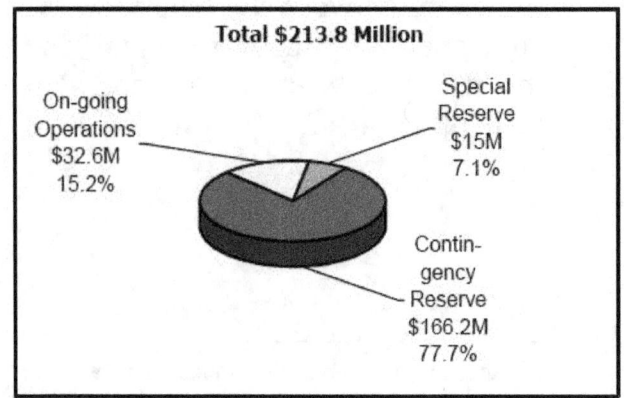

Part II – Financial Discussion and Analysis

Reserves

The *Special Reserve* serves to reduce the impact of unforecasted shortfalls or unbudgeted and unanticipated requirements. The *Contingency Reserve* funds foreseeable but rare events, such as a fire, flood, or impairment to the OCC's information technology network that may interfere with the OCC's ability to accomplish its mission. Both reserves are to be used at the discretion of the Comptroller. The OCC has also earmarked funds for on-going operations to cover undelivered orders, the consumption of assets, capital investments and district offices restructuring. Since the OCC does not receive congressional appropriations, the establishment of reserves is integral to the effective stewardship of its resources.

Statement of Net Cost

The *Statement of Net Cost* presents the full cost of operating the OCC's programs for the years ended September 30, 2002 and 2001. Costs are differentiated between those resulting from transactions between the OCC and other federal entities (intragovernmental) and transactions between the OCC and non-federal entities (with the public). The full cost includes an *Imputed Cost* of $17.7 million in FY 2002 and $15.4 million in FY 2001, the cost of the OCC's Federal Employees Retirement System (FERS) and Civil Service Retirement System (CSRS) plans, paid by the Office of Personnel Management (OPM). The

most significant line item is *Earned Revenues,* which increased by $26.8 million or 6.4 percent. As discussed under Funding Sources (page 37), this increase was primarily due to a rise in assessments collected during FY 2002.

Statement of Changes in Net Position

The *Statement of Changes in Net Position* presents the change in the OCC's net position resulting from the net cost of the OCC's operations and financing sources other than exchange revenues for the years ended September 30, 2002 and 2001. The most significant line item on the statement is the *Imputed financing from costs absorbed by others,* which increased by $2.3 million or 14.9 percent. The OCC's financing source resulted from a contribution of $15.4 million in FY 2001, and $17.7 million in FY 2002, by the OPM towards the OCC's FERS and CSRS retirement plans.

Statement of Budgetary Resources

The *Statement of Budgetary Resources* presents the budgetary resources available to the OCC, the status of these resources, and the net outlay of budgetary resources. The OCC obligated 57.2 percent of its available budgetary resources for the year. The remaining 42.8 percent was available primarily to cover the OCC's reserves.

Part II – Financial Discussion and Analysis

Statement of Financing

The *Statement of Financing* reconciles the resources available to the OCC to finance its operations with the net cost of operating its programs. A significant change in the statement from FY 2001 to FY 2002 was the $5.4 million difference in the *Change in Deferred Revenue.* The change in this line item was due to the increase in assessments collected during FY 2002.

Prompt Payment

The Prompt Payment Act and the OMB Circular A-125 require agencies to make payments on time, pay interest penalties when payments are late, and take discounts only when payments are made on or before the discount date. Figure 21 summarizes the OCC's prompt payment performance for FYs 2002 and 2001.

Figure 21: Prompt Payment Performance[3]

	FY 2002	FY 2001
Invoices paid	20,341	29,037
	$61,101,069	$93,465,199
Invoices paid late	484	587
	$4,683,467	$2,004,515
Interest penalties paid	238	104
	$7,403	$3,530

Electronic Funds Transfer

Using electronic funds transfer (EFT) for payments provides greater control over the timing of payments and reduces payment cost compared with paper checks. The Debt Collection Improvement Act of 1996 requires government agencies to issue all contractual and employee payments using EFT. Figure 22 summarizes EFT usage for FYs 2001 and 2002.

Figure 22: Electronic Funds Transfer Performance

	FY 2002	FY 2001
Vendor payments	99%	80%
Employee payments	100%	99.9%

---

[3] Number and dollar amount

Limitations to the Financial Statements

The financial statements have been prepared to report the assets, liabilities, and net position of the OCC and its net costs, changes in net position, budgetary resources, and reconciliation of net costs to budgetary obligations, pursuant to the requirements 31 USC 3515(b).

While the statements have been prepared from the books and records of the OCC in accordance with GAAP for federal entities and the formats prescribed by the OMB, the statements are in addition to the financial reports used to monitor and control budgetary resources that are prepared from the same books and records. The statements should be read with the realization that they are for a component of the U.S. Government, a sovereign entity.

SYSTEMS, CONTROLS, AND LEGAL COMPLIANCE

The Comptroller is required annually to provide a statement of assurance regarding the effectiveness of management, administrative, and accounting controls, and financial management systems. The FY 2002 Assurance Statement is exhibited on page 48.

In assessing the adequacy of management controls, the Comptroller relies on the judgment of senior executives, reports provided by the General Accounting Office (GAO), Treasury's OIG, the independent auditors, and internal quality assurance and program analyses conducted by the OCC's Program and Management Accountability Division. These sources provide a thorough and conscientious evaluation of the OCC's management control systems.

This section of the report provides the analytical basis of the Comptroller's assurance statement along with other information concerning the OCC's compliance with:

- Federal Managers' Financial Integrity Act,

- Federal Financial Management Improvement Act, and

- Other key legal and regulatory requirements.

Federal Managers' Financial Integrity Act of 1982

As discussed previously, the OCC implemented a financial and acquisitions management system that substantially complied with federal financial management systems requirements published by the JFMIP. Implementation of the system has remedied the limitations that caused last year's qualified assurance regarding FMFIA Section 4.

The OCC's management controls, as a whole, provide reasonable assurance that necessary management controls are in place and operating effectively, except that the OCC has not performed annual risk assessments as required by GISRA. The OCC is working to resolve the deficiency.

Federal Financial Management Improvement Act of 1995

Prior to FY 2002, the OCC's financial applications were composed of legacy systems, which were mainframe oriented and non-relational. This system was comprised of a mismatch of operating systems, databases, and interfaces, which were difficult to maintain and often impossible to modify.

With the implementation of the new financial and acquisitions management system, the OCC is in substantial compliance with FFMIA, because the new system:

Part II – Financial Discussion and Analysis

- Supports management's fiduciary role without requiring the adoption of extensive manual processes;

- Integrates the budget execution function in the core financial system with accounts payable, accounts receivable, and general ledger;

- Provides the users with on-line access to or daily reports on the status of funds to support the management and delivery of the OCC's programs and program decision-making; and

- Provides security over financial information in accordance with Circular A-130, Appendix 3 and supports internal controls over the financial system that are designed properly and operating effectively.

Government Information Security Reform Act of 2000

The OCC has not complied with the GISRA requirement to complete annual risk assessments for general support systems and applications. Several of the OCC's information systems subject to the GISRA were not evaluated in FY 2002. A formal corrective action plan with milestone dates is in place. Required risk assessments will be completed for general support systems before the end of CY 2002, and major applications in FY 2003.

Management Accountability Program

The OCC's management accountability program is managed independently of other programs to ensure that:

- Programs meet mission requirements,

- Resources are protected from waste, fraud, and mismanagement, and

- Activities comply with applicable laws and regulations.

The Program and Management Accountability Division reports directly to the Comptroller. Program objectives are accomplished through activities of the quality management, program analysis, and the OIG/GAO liaison functions.

- Quality Management ensures management accountability for establishing and maintaining cost-effective management controls and encourages organizational excellence through regular program reviews and other special studies to foster continuous organizational improvement.

- Program Analysis ensures strategic alignment of the OCC's programs and evaluates program efficiency and effectiveness.

- OIG/GAO Liaison facilitates audits, evaluations, and investigations and ensures managers take corrective action to recommendations.

Part II – Financial Discussion and Analysis

Management Control Review Program

The management control review program consists of an annual self-assessment for managers (SAM). The 2001 SAM revealed opportunities to improve controls in several areas. Senior management and the independent auditors determined, however, that none of the issues represent material weaknesses in the OCC's internal controls. Action plans are nonetheless in place for each area and implementation of proposed corrective actions is tracked.

In FY 2002, the SAM was administered to 192 managers representing five senior deputy comptroller areas. The 2002 SAM expanded on previous content to include assessments of planning, budgeting, and business resumption controls. The SAM results will be analyzed and corrective actions, as needed, will be tracked.

Continuity of Operations

The OCC's continuity of operations planning is sufficient to reduce risk to reasonable levels. In FY 2002, a review of the contingency plans was conducted to ensure the OCC is prepared to protect the workforce and maintain critical functions in the event of an emergency. The OCC established an Oversight Committee on Contingency Planning to direct revisions of the Continuity of Operations Plan (COOP). The revised COOP was submitted to the Department of the Treasury on April 26, 2002.

An independent analysis of the COOP by Treasury consultants found the OCC's plan to be satisfactory in all material aspects. The COOP formalizes and integrates information technology recovery plans, relocation scenarios, alternative site logistics, emergency communication procedures, lines of succession, and delegations of authority into a comprehensive emergency management plan.

Significant testing has been completed and continues on a regular basis for the various elements of the OCC's Information Technology Recovery Plan. All OCC managers received Emergency Preparedness and COOP Awareness training in FY 2002. In addition, the remaining employees will receive on-line training by the end of the calendar year.

Erroneous Payments

The prevention of erroneous payments is a key aspect of the OCC's financial management system and controls. The implementation of the new financial and acquisitions management system provides necessary discipline throughout all financial transaction processing.

Part II – Financial Discussion and Analysis

System implementation centralizes the disbursement function and results in stronger purchase controls. These controls allow the Comptroller to provide reasonable assurance that the OCC has sufficient controls to prevent erroneous payments. In addition, an internal audit by the Financial Management Division of 100 percent of the vendor file was completed in June 2002. This effort revealed no unauthorized vendors or improper payments.

Department of the Treasury
Office of the Comptroller of the Currency

Annual Assurance Statement
2002

The Office of the Comptroller of the Currency, as a whole, has made a conscientious effort during FY 2002 to meet the internal control requirements of the Federal Managers' Financial Integrity Act and the Federal Financial Management Information Act. As the Comptroller of the Currency, I recognize the importance of management controls and have taken the necessary measures to ensure a thorough evaluation of OCC's management control systems was completed during FY 2002. The results of this analysis indicate that the OCC's system of internal management, accounting and administrative control, taken as a whole, is sufficient and effective except that we have not completed the testing required to demonstrate compliance with the Government Information Security Reform Act of 2000. With this exception, I can provide reasonable assurance that FMFIA Section 2 and Section 4 objectives have been met. I am pleased to report substantial compliance with FFMIA resulting from implementation of OCC's new financial management system, which went live on October 1, 2001.

John D. Hawke, Jr.
Comptroller of the Currency

PART III

INDEPENDENT
AUDITORS' REPORT

2001 M Street, N.W.
Washington, D.C. 20036

Independent Auditors' Report on Financial Statements

The Comptroller of the Currency:

We have audited the accompanying balance sheets of the Office of the Comptroller of the Currency (OCC) as of September 30, 2002 and 2001, and the related statements of net cost, changes in net position, budgetary resources, and financing, for the years then ended. These financial statements are the responsibility of the OCC's management. Our responsibility is to express an opinion on these financial statements based on our audits.

We conducted our audits in accordance with auditing standards generally accepted in the United States of America; the standards applicable to financial audits contained in *Government Auditing Standards*, issued by the Comptroller General of the United States; and Office of Management and Budget (OMB) Bulletin No. 01-02, *Audit Requirements for Federal Financial Statements*. Those standards and OMB Bulletin No. 01-02 require that we plan and perform the audits to obtain reasonable assurance about whether the financial statements are free of material misstatement. An audit includes examining, on a test basis, evidence supporting the amounts and disclosures in the financial statements. An audit also includes assessing the accounting principles used and significant estimates made by management, as well as evaluating the overall financial statement presentation. We believe that our audits provide a reasonable basis for our opinion.

In our opinion, the financial statements referred to above present fairly, in all material respects, the financial position of the OCC, as of September 30, 2002 and 2001, and its net costs, changes in net position, budgetary resources, and reconciliation of net costs to budgetary obligations for the years then ended, in conformity with accounting principles generally accepted in the United States of America.

The information in Management's Discussion and Analysis is not a required part of the financial statements but is supplementary information required by accounting principles generally accepted in the United States of America. We have applied certain limited procedures, which consisted principally of inquiries of management regarding the methods of measurement and presentation of this information. However, we did not audit this information and, accordingly, we express no opinion on it.

KPMG LLP. KPMG LLP, a U.S. limited liability partnership, is a member of KPMG International, a Swiss association.

51

Our audit was conducted for the purpose of forming an opinion on the financial statements taken as a whole. The supplementary information included in Appendices A and B is presented for purposes of additional analysis and is not a required part of the financial statements. We did not audit this information and, accordingly, we express no opinion on it.

In accordance with *Government Auditing Standards*, we have also issued reports dated November 1, 2002, on our consideration of the OCC's internal control over financial reporting and its compliance with certain provisions of laws and regulations. Those reports are an integral part of an audit performed in accordance with *Government Auditing Standards*, and should be read in conjunction with this report in considering the results of our audits.

November 1, 2002

2001 M Street, N.W.
Washington, D.C. 20036

Independent Auditors' Report on Internal Control over Financial Reporting

The Comptroller of the Currency:

We have audited the balance sheets of the Office of the Comptroller of the Currency (OCC) as of September 30, 2002 and 2001, and the related statements of net cost, changes in net position, budgetary resources, and financing, for the years then ended, and have issued our report thereon dated November 1, 2002. We conducted our audits in accordance with auditing standards generally accepted in the United States of America; the standards applicable to financial audits contained in *Government Auditing Standards*, issued by the Comptroller General of the United States; and Office of Management and Budget (OMB) Bulletin No. 01-02, *Audit Requirements for Federal Financial Statements*.

In planning and performing our fiscal year 2002 audit, we considered the OCC's internal control over financial reporting by obtaining an understanding of the OCC's internal control, determining whether internal controls had been placed in operation, assessing control risk, and performing tests of controls in order to determine our auditing procedures for the purpose of expressing our opinion on the financial statements. We limited our internal control testing to those controls necessary to achieve the objectives described in OMB Bulletin No. 01-02 and *Government Auditing Standards*. We did not test all internal controls relevant to operating objectives as broadly defined by the Federal Managers' Financial Integrity Act of 1982. The objective of our audit was not to provide assurance on the OCC's internal control over financial reporting. Consequently, we do not provide an opinion thereon.

Our consideration of internal control over financial reporting would not necessarily disclose all matters in the internal control over financial reporting that might be reportable conditions. Under standards issued by the American Institute of Certified Public Accountants, reportable conditions are matters coming to our attention relating to significant deficiencies in the design or operation of the internal control over financial reporting that, in our judgment, could adversely affect the OCC's ability to record, process, summarize, and report financial data consistent with the assertions by management in the financial statements. Material weaknesses are reportable conditions in which the design or operation of one or more of the internal control components does not reduce to a relatively low level the risk that misstatements, in amounts that would be material in relation to the financial statements being audited,

KPMG LLP. KPMG LLP, a U.S. limited liability partnership, is
a member of KPMG International, a Swiss association.

53

may occur and not be detected within a timely period by employees in the normal course of performing their assigned functions. Because of inherent limitations in any internal control, misstatements due to error or fraud may occur and not be detected.

In our fiscal year 2002 audit, we noted one matter, discussed in Exhibit I, involving the internal control over financial reporting and its operation that we consider to be a reportable condition. However, this reportable condition is not believed to be a material weakness. Exhibit II presents the status of prior year reportable conditions.

Additional Required Procedures

As required by OMB Bulletin No. 01-02, with respect to internal control related to performance measures determined by management to be key and reported in the Management's Discussion and Analysis section of the OCC's Annual Report, we obtained an understanding of the design of significant internal controls relating to the existence and completeness assertions. Our procedures were not designed to provide assurance on internal control over reported performance measures, and, accordingly, we do not provide an opinion thereon.

_____

We also noted other matters involving internal control and its operation that we have reported to the management of the OCC in a separate letter dated November 1, 2002.

This report is intended solely for the information and use of the OCC's management, the Department of the Treasury Office of Inspector General, OMB, and Congress and is not intended to be and should not be used by anyone other than these specified parties.

November 1, 2002

Exhibit I

Office of the Comptroller of the Currency
Reportable Condition
For the Fiscal Year Ended September 30, 2002 Audit

1. *$MART System Controls Should be Strengthened*

IT Audit Area	Condition	Recommendation
Application Security Controls	Administrator and user access privileges for the $MART Core Financial Management System (CFMS) are not assigned in accordance with the "Least Privilege" principle.	Establish procedures for the administration of $MART user accounts, including the establishment of new accounts, the edits/updates made to existing accounts, and the deletion of accounts. These procedures should include the requirement that the issuance of access privileges, both new and updated, be justified by job function and approved by an authorized individual. Create a database log that accurately depicts the current class assignments for $MART users, and establish procedures for the review of this log by Security Administrators for the maintenance of user accounts and the detection of changes made to access privileges. Restrict the number of individuals assigned to high-level privilege classes for security administration of the $MART system. Delete or disable default ID. Since we brought these issues to OCC management's attention, corrective action has been taken.
Infrastructure Security	Entity-wide security program documentation is incomplete. Specifically, risk assessments for general support systems and major applications have not been completed and the $MART security plan contains inaccurate control descriptions.	The OCC's management should continue its efforts in implementing an entity-wide security program by performing system based risk assessments using NIST Special Publication 800-26 for each mission critical/major system, developing and/or updating security plans based on these risk assessments, and performing the necessary system certifications and accreditations in accordance with OMB A-130. Due to competing priorities, the OCC's management was not able to complete the risk assessments in fiscal year 2002. However, the OCC plans to complete the risk assessments during fiscal year 2003.

Exhibit I (continued)

Office of the Comptroller of the Currency
Reportable Condition
For the Fiscal Year Ended September 30, 2002 Audit

1. $MART System Controls Should be Strengthened (continued)

IT Audit Area	Condition	Recommendation
IT Operational Controls	Documentation supporting requests, program changes, testing, and acceptance for the $MART system needs to be improved. Specifically, information should be recorded to provide evidence for authorization of the change request, testing of the program change, and approval of the change for migration into production.	The OCC's management should ensure that a process exists to document each program change user authorization, developer and user testing, and user approval to migrate the program change into production. In addition, roles should be established as part of a change control environment, whereby developers, administrators migrating source code, and users are properly segregated. The OCC's management is taking steps to address this issue and should have it resolved during fiscal year 2003.
IT Operational Controls	Disaster recovery capabilities for the $MART system have not been tested.	The OCC's management should ensure that recovery capabilities for the $MART system are clearly established within the Information Technology Recovery Plan and the Continuity of Operations Plan, and that tests of these capabilities are performed to ensure that they are effective. The results of these tests should be used to generate planning improvements that will increase the OCC's ability to recover. The OCC's management plans to address this issue in fiscal year 2003.

Exhibit II

Office of the Comptroller of the Currency
Status of Prior Year Reportable Conditions

2001 Reportable Conditions	2002 Status
Adequate controls over Time and Travel Reports (TTRS) disbursements were not in place. *(OCC did not consistently follow procedures related to TTRS disbursements.)*	Improvements noted and downgraded to a management letter comment. Prior year exceptions included missing supervisory approvals and TTRS disbursements prior to authorization for payment. Current year exceptions related to disbursements prior to authorization; however, they occurred less frequently, were related to remotely located personnel, and occurred prior to the OCC policy change facilitating the authorization process.
Internal controls over timekeeping were not adequate *(OCC did not consistently follow timekeeping procedures.)*	Improvements noted and downgraded to a management letter comment. The nature of the prior year errors included inadequate and untimely leave slip and certifying roster approvals, and inaccurate certifying rosters. Current year exceptions related to untimely leave slip approvals by individuals charging annual leave when sick leave is not available and one instance of inadequate certifying roster approval.

2001 M Street, N.W.
Washington, D.C. 20036

Independent Auditors' Report on Compliance with Laws and Regulations

The Comptroller of the Currency:

We have audited the balance sheets of the Office of the Comptroller of the Currency (OCC) as of September 30, 2002 and 2001, and the related statements of net cost, changes in net position, budgetary resources, and financing, for the years then ended, and have issued our report thereon dated November 1, 2002. We conducted our audits in accordance with auditing standards generally accepted in the United States of America; the standards applicable to financial audits contained in *Government Auditing Standards,* issued by the Comptroller General of the United States; and Office of Management and Budget (OMB) Bulletin No. 01-02, *Audit Requirements for Federal Financial Statements.*

The management of the OCC is responsible for complying with laws and regulations applicable to the OCC. As part of obtaining reasonable assurance about whether the OCC's financial statements are free of material misstatement, we performed tests of the OCC's compliance with certain provisions of laws and regulations, noncompliance with which could have a direct and material effect on the determination of the financial statement amounts, and certain provisions of other laws and regulations specified in OMB Bulletin No. 01-02, including certain requirements referred to in the Federal Financial Management Improvement Act (FFMIA) of 1996. We limited our tests of compliance to the provisions described in the preceding sentence, and we did not test compliance with all laws and regulations applicable to the OCC. However, providing an opinion on compliance with laws and regulations was not an objective of our audit, and, accordingly, we do not express such an opinion.

The results of our tests of compliance with certain provisions of laws and regulations described in the preceding paragraph, exclusive of FFMIA, disclosed no instances of noncompliance that are required to be reported under *Government Auditing Standards* and OMB Bulletin No. 01-02.

Under FFMIA, we are required to report whether the OCC's financial management systems substantially comply with (1) Federal financial management systems requirements, (2) applicable Federal accounting standards, and (3) the United States Government Standard General Ledger at the transaction level. To meet this

requirement, we performed tests of compliance with FFMIA Section 803(a) requirements.

The results of our tests disclosed no instances in which the OCC's financial management systems did not substantially comply with the three requirements discussed in the preceding paragraph.

This report is intended solely for the information and use of the OCC's management, the Department of the Treasury Office of Inspector General, OMB, and Congress and is not intended to be and should not be used by anyone other than these specified parties.

November 1, 2002

PART IV

FINANCIAL STATEMENTS
AND NOTES

Part IV – Financial Statements and Notes

Office of the Comptroller of the Currency
Balance Sheets
As of September 30, 2002 and 2001

	FY 2002	FY 2001
Assets:		
Intragovernmental:		
Fund balance with Treasury	$ 2,102,0 24	$ 546,160
Investments and related interest (Note 3)	387,918,5 77	349,923,315
Advances and prepayments	11,475	256,185
Total intragovernmental	390,032,0 76	350,725,6 60
Cash	26,092	26,092
Accounts receivable, net	347,191	293,127
Property and equipment, net (Note 4)	25,056,2 25	18,860,3 98
Advances and prepayments	1,610,2 44	1,971,5 73
Total Assets	**$ 417,071,828**	**$ 371,876,850**
Liabilities:		
Intragovernmental:		
Accounts payable	$ 825,485	$ 1,905,5 91
Total intragovernmental	**825,485**	**1,905,591**
Accounts payable	13,699,4 36	7,544,6 02
Accrued payroll and employee benefits	10,986,038	19,993,1 42
Deferred revenue (Note 5)	109,745,7 35	100,244,7 84
Accrued annual leave	21,954,0 61	20,855,5 76
Post retirement benefit (Note 7)	8,183,0 25	7,563,9 45
Total liabilities	**165,393,780**	**158,107,640**
Net position (Note 8)	**$ 251,678,048**	**$ 213,769,210**
Total Liabilities and Net Position	**$ 417,071,828**	**$ 371,876,850**

The accompanying notes are an integral part of these financial statements.

Part IV – Financial Statements and Notes

Office of the Comptroller of the Currency
Statements of Net Cost
For the Years Ended September 30, 2002 and 2001

	FY 2002	FY 2001
Program Costs:		
Intragovernmental	$ 58,768,603	$ 58,011,797
With the public	363,651,090	362,107,646
Total program costs (Note 9)	422,419,693	420,119,443
Less: Earned revenues	(442,655,111)	(415,875,984)
Net Cost of Operations	$ (20,235,418)	$ 4,243,459

The accompanying notes are an integral part of these financial statements.

Part IV – Financial Statements and Notes

Office of the Comptroller of the Currency
Statements of Changes in Net Position
For the Years Ended September 30, 2002 and 2001

	FY 2002	FY 2001
Beginning Balances	$ 213,769,2 10	$ 213,992,8 12
Prior Period Adjustment (Note 4)	-	(11,419,7 31)
Beginning balances, as adjusted	213,769,2 10	202,573,0 81
Other Financing Sources:		
Imputed financing from costs absorbed by others (Note 7)	17,673,4 20	15,439,588
Net Cost of Operations	20,235,4 18	(4,243,4 59)
Ending Balances	$ 251,678,048	$ 213,769,210

The accompanying notes are an integral part of these financial statements.

Part IV – Financial Statements and Notes

Office of the Comptroller of the Currency
Statements of Budgetary Resources
For the Years Ended September 30, 2002 and 2001

	FY 2002	FY 2001
Budgetary Resources:		
Unobligated balance:		
Beginning of Period	$ 281,479,230	$ 268,658,850
Spending Authority from offsetting collections:		
Earned		
Collected	448,885,271	417,011,484
Receivable from Federal Sources	(204,323)	2,142,917
Subtotal	448,680,948	419,154,401
Total Budgetary Resources	$ 730,160,178	$ 687,813,251
Status of Budgetary Resources:		
Obligations incurred	417,402,529	406,334,021
Unobligated balance available	312,757,649	281,479,230
Total Status of Budgetary Resources	730,160,178	687,813,251
Relationship of Obligations to Outlays:		
Obligated Balance, net, beginning of period	63,078,883	59,749,322
Obligated Balance, net, end of period:		
Interest Receivable	(4,891,458)	(5,095,781)
Undelivered Orders	17,378,278	10,311,809
Accounts Payable and Accruals, net of assessment		
refunds	54,828,210	57,862,855
Outlays:		
Disbursements	413,370,706	400,861,543
Collections	(448,885,271)	(417,011,484)
Net Collections in Excess of Disbursements	$ (35,514,565)	$ (16,149,941)

The accompanying notes are an integral part of these financial statements.

Part IV – Financial Statements and Notes

Office of the Comptroller of the Currency
Statements of Financing
For the Years Ended September 30, 2002 and 2001

	FY 2002	FY 2001
Resources Used to Finance Activities:		
Budgetary Resources Obligated		
Obligations Incurred	$ 417,402,529	$ 406,334,021
Less: Spending authority from offsetting collections	(448,680,948)	(419,154,401)
Net obligations	(31,278,419)	(12,820,380)
Other Resources		
Imputed financing from costs absorbed by others (Note 7)	17,673,420	15,439,588
Total resources used to finance activities	**(13,604,999)**	**2,619,208**
Resources Used to Finance Items not Part of the		
Net Cost of Operations		
Change in budgetary resources obligated for goods, services and		
benefits ordered but not yet provided	(6,460,430)	397,749
Resources that finance the acquisition of assets	(11,474,517)	(6,045,753)
Other resources or adjustments to net obligated resources that		
do not affect net cost of operations	(54,064)	(169,054)
Total resources used to finance items not part of the		
net cost of operations	**(17,989,011)**	**(5,817,058)**
Total resources used to finance the net cost of		
operations	**(31,594,010)**	**(3,197,850)**
Components of the Net Cost of Operations that will not		
Require or Generate Resources in the Current Period:		
Components Requiring or Generating Resources in Future Periods:		
Change in Deferred Revenue	9,500,951	4,094,784
Assessment Refunds	819,836	-
Total components of net cost of operations that will		
require or generate resources in future periods	10,320,787	4,094,784
Components not Requiring or Generating Resources:		
Decrease in Accumulated Depreciation	5,209,402	3,948,481
Net Increase in Bond Premium	(4,240,884)	(662,637)
Other	69,287	60,681
Total components of Net Cost of Operations that will not		
require or generate resources	1,037,805	3,346,525
Total components of Net Cost of Operations that will not		
require or generate resources in the current period	**11,358,592**	**7,441,309**
Net Cost of Operations	**$ (20,235,418)**	**$ 4,243,459**

The accompanying notes are an integral part of these financial statements.

Part IV – Financial Statements and Notes

Note 1 - Organization

The OCC was created as a bureau within the U.S. Department of the Treasury by an act of Congress in 1863. The OCC was created for the purpose of establishing and regulating a system of federally chartered national banks. The National Currency Act of 1863, rewritten and reenacted as the National Bank Act of 1864, authorized the OCC to supervise national banks and to regulate the lending and investment activities of federally chartered institutions.

The OCC's revenue is derived primarily from assessments and fees paid by national banks and income on investments in U.S. Government securities. The OCC does not receive Congressional appropriations to fund any of its operations. Therefore, the OCC does not have any unexpended appropriations.

By federal statute 12 USC § 481, the OCC's funds are maintained in a U.S. Government trust revolving fund. The funds remain available to cover the annual costs of the OCC's operations in accordance with policies established by the Comptroller.

The OCC collects Civil Monetary Penalties (CMP) due to the federal government that are assessed through court enforced legal actions against a national bank and/or its officers. CMP collections transferred to the Department's General Fund amounted to $10,175,092 in FY 2002, and $159,016 in FY 2001. The increase was primarily due to a one-time penalty assessment. Outstanding CMPs at September 30, 2002 and 2001, amounted to $1,218,534 and $785,258, respectively.

The Departmental Offices (DO), another entity of the U.S. Department of the Treasury, provides certain administrative services to the OCC. The OCC pays the DO for services rendered pursuant to established interagency agreements. Administrative services provided by the DO totaled $2,081,306 in FY 2002, and $2,765,467 in FY 2001.

Part IV – Financial Statements and Notes

Note 2 - Significant Accounting Policies

Basis of Accounting

The OCC's financial statements have been prepared from the OCC's accounting records in conformity with accounting principles generally accepted in the United States of America (GAAP). The financial statements consist of a balance sheet, and the statements of net cost, changes in net position, budgetary resources, and financing. These financial statements are presented on a comparative basis providing information for FYs 2002 and 2001.

The financial statements reflect both the accrual and budgetary bases of accounting. Under the accrual method, revenues are recognized when earned and expenses are recognized when a liability is incurred, without regard to cash receipt or payment. The budgetary method recognizes the obligation of funds according to legal requirements, which, in many cases, is made prior to the occurrence of an accrual-based transaction. Budgetary accounting is essential for compliance with legal constraints and controls over the use of federal funds.

Fund Balance with Treasury

The OCC's cash receipts and disbursements are processed by the U.S. Treasury. Sufficient funds are maintained in a U.S. Government trust revolving fund and are available to pay current liabilities. The OCC invests all the funds that are not immediately needed in U.S. Government securities (Note 3).

Accounts Receivable, net

Accounts receivable represent monies owed to the OCC for services and goods provided. Accounts receivable are reduced to their net realizable value by an Allowance for Doubtful Accounts. The OCC reserves an allowance equal to 100 percent of accounts with outstanding balances exceeding one year, and 50 percent of accounts with balances exceeding six months but less than one year. At September 30, 2002 and 2001, accounts receivable amounted to $366,215 less an allowance of $19,024, and $312,171 less and allowance of $19,044, respectively.

Part IV – Financial Statements and Notes

Advances and Prepayments

Advances and prepayments to other government agencies represent amounts paid to the DO prior to the receipt of goods and services. Advances and prepayments to the public consist of rent and insurance paid. The amounts are recorded as prepaid expenses at the time of payment and are expensed when related goods and services are received.

Liabilities

Liabilities represent the amounts owing or accruing under contractual or other arrangements governing the transactions, including operating expenses incurred but not yet paid. Payments are made in a timely manner in accordance with the Prompt Payment Act. Interest penalties are paid when payments are late. Discounts are taken when cost effective and the invoice is paid by the discount date.

Annual, Sick, and Other Leave

Annual leave is accrued and funded by the OCC as it is earned, and the accrual is reduced as leave is taken or paid. Each year, the balance in the accrued annual leave account is adjusted to reflect current pay rates. Sick leave and other types of leave are expended as taken.

Use of Estimates

The preparation of financial statements, in accordance with GAAP, requires management to make estimates and assumptions that affect the reported amounts of assets and liabilities, the disclosure of contingent assets and liabilities at the date of the financial statements, and the reported amounts of revenue and expenses during the reporting period. Such estimates and assumptions could change in the future as more information becomes known, which could impact the amounts reported and disclosed herein.

Part IV – Financial Statements and Notes

Note 3 - Investments and Related Interest

Investments are U.S. Treasury securities stated at amortized cost and the related accrued interest. The OCC plans to hold these investments to maturity. Premiums and discounts are amortized over the term of the investment using the straight-line method, which approximates the effective yield method. The fair market value of investment securities was $392,537,740 at September 30, 2002, and $350,441,058 at September 30, 2001.

Investments and Related Interest Receivable

	FY 2002	FY 2001
Cost	$378,468,000	$344,722,000
Net Unamortized Premium	4,559,119	105,534
Net Amortized Value	383,027,1 19	344,827,5 34
Interest Receivable	4,891,458	5,095,781
Total	**$387,918,577**	**$349,923,315**

FY 2002 Investment Portfolio

Maturity	Par Value	Coupon Rate
Overnight	$134,468,000	1.900%
During 2002	80,000,000	5.750%
During 2003	55,000,000	4.250%
During 2004	55,000,000	5.875%
During 2005	29,000,000	5.750%
During 2006	25,000,000	6.875%
Total	**$378,468,000**	

FY 2001 Investment Portfolio

Maturity	Par Value	Coupon Rate
Overnight	$ 90,722,000	3.180%[4]
During 2001	149,000,000	5.875%
During 2002	80,000,000	5.750%
During 2006	25,000,000	6.875%
Total	**$344,722,000**	

---

[4] The coupon rate for the FY 2001 overnight investments was updated from the prior year.

Part IV – Financial Statements and Notes

Note 4 - Property and Equipment, net

Property and equipment purchased at a cost greater than or equal to the noted thresholds below with useful lives of five years or more are capitalized at cost and depreciated or amortized, as applicable.

Leasehold improvements are amortized on a straight-line basis over the lesser of the terms of the related leases or their estimated useful lives. All other property and equipment are depreciated or amortized, as applicable, on a straight-line basis over their estimated useful lives. The tables presented below summarize property and equipment balances as of September 30, 2002, and 2001.

FY 2002 Property and Equipment, net

Class of Assets	Capitalization Threshold/ Useful Life		Cost	Accumulated Depreciation	Net Book Value
Leasehold Improvements	$50,000	5-20	$23,283,734	$(14,357,099)	$8,926,635
Equipment	50,000	5-10	6,414,633	(4,193,900)	2,220,733
Furniture and Fixtures	50,000	5-10	1,035,514	(723,252)	312,262
Internal Use Software	500,000	5-10	13,248,076	(3,357,885)	9,890,191
Internal Use Software-Dev	500,000	5-10	3,706,404	-	3,706,404
Total			**$47,688,361**	**$(22,632,136)**	**$25,056,225**

FY 2001 Property and Equipment, net

Class of Assets	Capitalization Threshold/ Useful Life		Cost	Accumulated Depreciation	Net Book Value
Leasehold Improvements	$50,000	5-20	$22,164,561	$(11,776,363)	$10,388,198
Equipment	50,000	5-10	11,369,857	(8,331,805)	3,038,052
Furniture and Fixtures	50,000	5-10	1,723,156	(1,230,193)	492,963
Internal Use Software	500,000	5-10	5,059,129	(2,021,763)	3,037,366
Internal Use Software-Dev	500,000	5-10	1,903,819	-	1,903,819
Total			**$42,220,522**	**$(23,360,124)**	**$18,860,398**

The OCC adopted the provisions of Statement of Federal Financial Accounting Standards No. 10, *Accounting for Internal Use Software,* effective October 1, 2000, which represented a change in accounting principle. The OCC followed the U.S. Department of Treasury's guidance for the implementation of the standard. The effect of the change in FY 2001 was a write-off of $11,419,731 of costs capitalized in prior years.

Note 5 - Deferred Revenue

The OCC's activities are primarily financed by assessments on assets held by national banks and the federal branches of foreign banks. These assessments are due January 31 and July 31 of each year based on asset balances as of call dates on December 31 and June 30, respectively. Assessments are paid in advance and are recognized as earned revenue on a straight-line basis over the six months following the call date. The unearned portions are reduced accordingly.

Part IV – Financial Statements and Notes

Note 6 - Leases

The OCC leases office space for headquarters operations in Washington, D.C., and for district and field operations through the General Services Administration of the U.S. Government. The lease agreements expire at various dates through 2009. These leases are treated as operating leases. In FY 2002, operating lease payments decreased due to office consolidations.

FY 2002 Future Lease Payments

Year	Amount
2003	$22,333,599
2004	19,126,850
2005	17,131,332
2006	11,491,191
2007	2,408,777
2008 and beyond	6,850,754
Total	**$79,342,503**

FY 2001 Future Lease Payments

Year	Amount
2002	$23,425,454
2003	20,417,635
2004	17,245,985
2005	15,178,776
2006	9,541,736
2007 and beyond	932,790
Total	**$86,742,376**

Part IV – Financial Statements and Notes

Note 7 - Retirement Plans and Other Benefits

Retirement

The OCC's employees are eligible to participate in one of two retirement plans. Employees hired prior to January 1, 1984, are covered by the CSRS unless they elected to join the FERS and Social Security during the election period. Employees hired after December 31, 1983, are automatically covered by FERS and Social Security. For employees covered by CSRS, the OCC contributes 8.51 percent of their adjusted base pay to the plan. For employees covered by FERS, the OCC contributes 10.7 percent of their adjusted base salary. The OCC's contributions totaled $13,490,210 in FY 2002, and $20,551,397 in FY 2001. Furthermore, the OPM contributed an additional $17,673,420 towards these retirement plans during FY 2002, and $15,439,588 in FY 2001. The OCC recognized these contributions as "Imputed Costs Absorbed by Others" and an offset in equal amount to "Imputed Financing from Costs Absorbed by Others" as a result of not having to reimburse the OPM.

The OCC does not report in its financial statements information pertaining to the retirement plans covering its employees. Reporting amounts such as plan assets, accumulated plan benefits, or unfunded liabilities, if any, are presently the responsibility of the OPM.

Other Benefits

The OCC's employees are eligible to participate in the Federal Thrift Savings Plan (TSP). For those employees under FERS, a TSP account is automatically established, and the OCC contributes a mandatory one percent of adjusted base pay to this account. In addition, the OCC matches employee contributions up to an additional four percent of pay, for a maximum OCC contribution amounting to five percent of adjusted base pay. Employees under CSRS may participate in the TSP, but do not receive the OCC automatic (one percent) and matching employer contributions. The OCC's contributions for the TSP totaled $5,749,904 in FY 2002, and $5,304,214 in FY 2001. The OCC also contributed a total of $11,045,830 for Social Security and Medicare benefits for all eligible employees in FY 2002, and $10,558,496 in FY 2001.

Employees can elect to contribute up to 10 percent of their adjusted base salary in the OCC 401(K) Plan, subject to Internal Revenue regulations. Prudential Securities Incorporated currently administers the plan. The OCC contributes a fixed one percent of the adjusted base salary to the Plan for all participating employees. Approximately 2,400 employees are currently enrolled in the plan,

Part IV – Financial Statements and Notes

which represents a participation rate exceeding 85 percent. The total cost of the OCC's one percent matching contribution plus associated administration fees amounted to $2,079,283 during FY 2002, and $1,863,769 in FY 2001.

The OCC sponsors a life insurance benefit plan for current and former employees. This plan is a defined benefit plan. Premium payments made during FY 2002 totaled $110,524, and $110,595 in FY 2001.

Accrued Post-Retirement Benefit Cost and Net Periodic Post-Retirement Benefit Cost

Component	FY 2002	FY 2001
Accumulated Post-Retirement Benefit Obligation	$(9,094,149)	$(7,303,739)
Unrecognized Transition Obligation	1,728,382	1,901,219
Unrecognized Net Gain	(817,258)	(2,161,425)
Total	**$(8,183,025)**	**$(7,563,945)**
Service Cost	$311,064	$294,498
Interest Cost	527,384	496,830
Amortization of Gain	(136,536)	(139,829)
Amortization of Transition Obligation	172,837	172,837
Total	**$874,749**	**$824,336**

The weighted-average discount rate used in determining the accumulated post-retirement benefit obligation was 7.5 percent. Gains or losses due to changes in actuarial assumptions are amortized over the service life of the plan.

Employees and retirees of the OCC are eligible to participate in Federal Employees Health Benefits (FEHB) and Federal Employees Group Life Insurance (FEGLI) plans that involve a cost sharing of bi-weekly coverage premiums by employee and employer. Both of these employee benefit plans are administered by the OPM. Total OCC contributions for active employees who participate in the FEHB plans were $11,319,414 for FY 2002, and $10,103,674 for FY 2001. The OCC's contributions for active employees who participate in the FEGLI plan were $196,516 for FY 2002, and $184,792 for FY 2001.

The Federal Employees' Compensation Act (FECA) provides income and medical cost protection to covered federal civilian employees injured on the job, employees who have incurred a work-related occupational disease, and beneficiaries of employees whose death is attributable to a job-related injury or occupational disease. Claims incurred for benefits for the OCC's employees under FECA are administered by the U.S. Department of Labor (DOL) and later billed to the OCC. The OCC accrued $4,390,674 of workers' compensation costs as of September 30, 2002, and $4,111,801 as of September 30, 2001. This amount includes unpaid costs and an actuarial estimated liability for unbilled costs incurred as of year-end calculated by the DOL.

Part IV – Financial Statements and Notes

Note 8 - Net Position

The OCC sets aside a portion of its Net Position as Special and Contingency Reserves to be used at the discretion of the Comptroller. In addition, funds are set aside to cover on-going cost of operations.

The Special Reserve supplements revenue from assessments and other sources that are made available to fund the OCC's annual budget. The Special Reserve serves to reduce the impact on operations of unforecasted revenue shortfalls or unbudgeted and unanticipated requirements or opportunities.

The Contingency Reserve supports the OCC's ability to accomplish its mission in the case of unforeseeable but rare events. Unforeseeable but rare events are beyond the control of the OCC, such as a major change in the national banking system or a disaster such as a fire, flood, or significant impairment of its information technology systems.

Net Position Availability

Component	FY 2002	FY 2001
Contingency Reserve	$178,554,013	$166,234,445
Special Reserve	15,000,000	15,000,000
Earmarked for On-going Operations:		
Undelivered Orders	17,378,278	10,311,809
Consumption of Assets	32,107,691	22,222,956
Capital Investments	6,138,066	-
District Offices Restructuring	2,500,000	-
Net Position	**$251,678,048**	**$213,769,210**

Part IV – Financial Statements and Notes

Note 9 - Program Costs

The implementation of $MART in FY 2002 enabled the OCC to capture costs by program. The following table differentiates program costs resulting from transactions between the OCC and other federal entities (intragovernmental) and transactions between the OCC and non-federal entities (with the public).

Program Costs	FY 2002
Supervise Program	
Intragovernmental	$50,142,410
With the public	310,273,531
Total Program Costs	360,415,941
Charter Program	
Intragovernmental	1,574,820
With the public	9,744,747
Total Program Costs	11,319,567
Regulate Program	
Intragovernmental	3,472,050
With the public	21,484,513
Total Program Costs	24,956,563
Analyze Risk Program	
Intragovernmental	3,579,323
With the public	22,148,299
Total Program Costs	25,727,622
Total	422,419,693
Less: Earned revenues	(442,655,111)
Net Cost of Operations	**$(20,235,418)**

Part IV – Financial Statements and Notes

Note 10 - Expenses by Budget Object Classification

The following table illustrates the OCC's costs by major budget object class for FYs 2002 and 2001.

Budget Object Class	FY 2002	FY 2001
Personnel Compensation	$232,359,148	$ 223,923,416
Personnel Benefits	60,160,137	58,352,700
Benefits to Former Employees	520,099	2,112,678
Travel and Transportation of Persons	25,393,310	24,741,781
Travel and Transportation of Things	830,647	1,019,015
Rent, Communication, and Utilities	33,449,836	36,484,468
Printing and Reproduction	929,212	1,074,570
Other Contractual Services	37,708,589	40,858,089
Supplies and Materials	2,253,706	3,528,000
Equipment	5,548,567	7,830,554
Land and Structures	349,433	608,371
Insurance Claims and Indemnities	34,187	197,731
Depreciation	5,209,402	3,948,482
Imputed Costs	17,673,420	15,439,588
Total	**$422,419,693**	**$420,119,443**

Note 11 - Contingencies

The OCC is reviewing potential contingencies, which may result from the effect of certain policies and procedures currently in place. In the opinion of the OCC's management and legal counsel, the ultimate results of these potential contingencies will not materially affect the financial statements of the OCC.

Appendix A – FY 2002 Performance Measures and Results

The OCC's FY 2002 performance measures, customer service standards, and results are presented below.

OCC Program	Performance Measure Customer Service Standard	CY 1999 Performance	CY 2000 Performance	FY 2001 Performance	FY 2002 Target	FY 2002 Performance	FY 2003 Plan
	Strategic Goal 1: A safe and sound national banking system						
	Percent of large and mid-size banks where quarterly risk assessments are completed	Not Applicable	Not Applicable	Not Applicable	100%	100%	Discontinued (Note A)
	Percent of large and mid-size banks that received an annual report of examination	Not Applicable	Not Applicable	Not Applicable	100%	97%[1]	Discontinued (Note A)
	Percent of community bank examinations conducted in accordance with the FDICIA-mandated schedule, exclusive of approved exceptions	92%	98%	94%	100%	98%[2]	Discontinued (Note A)
Supervise	Percent of community bank examinations that are approved exceptions to the FDICIA-mandated schedule	Not Applicable	Not Applicable	Not Applicable	≤ 10%	3%	Discontinued (Note A)
	Average calendar days past due on community bank examinations that do not meet the approved exception criteria	Not Applicable	Not Applicable	Not Applicable	≤ 15	17[3]	Discontinued (Note A)
	The examiner's requests for information before and during the examination were reasonable and justified by the examination scope. (Note B)	Not Applicable	1.36	1.36	≤ 1.75	1.36	≤ 1.75

○ **Performance and Accountability Report – FY 2002**

Appendix A – FY 2002 Performance Measures and Results

OCC Program	Performance Measure Customer Service Standard	CY 1999 Performance	CY 2000 Performance	FY 2001 Performance	FY 2002 Target	FY 2002 Performance	FY 2003 Plan
	The examination team conducted the examination in a professional manner. (Note B)	Not Applicable	1.22	1.21	≤ 1.75	1.21	≤ 1.75
	During exit and board meetings, the examiner-in-charge and examination team clearly and effectively communicated their findings and concerns. (Note B)	Not Applicable	1.30	1.33	≤ 1.75	1.32	≤ 1.75
Supervise	The report of examination clearly communicated examination findings, significant issues and the corrective actions (including timeframes) management and/or the board needed to take. (Note B)	Not Applicable	1.32	1.31	≤ 1.75	1.30	≤ 1.75
	On-going communication by the examiner-in-charge with senior management and/or the board was appropriate. (Note B)	Not Applicable	1.29	1.29	≤ 1.75	1.29	≤ 1.75
Strategic Goal 2: A flexible legal and regulatory framework that enables the national banking system to provide a full competitive array of financial services							
	Percent of corporate applications processed on-time	≥ 95%	96%	96%	95%	96%	95%
Charter	Average rating of timeliness of decisions (Note C)	1.26	1.22	1.15	≤ 1.5	1.19	≤ 1.5
	Average rating of knowledge of OCC staff (Note C)	1.20	1.16	1.17	≤ 1.5	1.19	≤ 1.5
	Average rating of professionalism of OCC staff (Note C)	1.12	1.11	1.10	≤ 1.5	1.12	≤ 1.5

○ **Performance and Accountability Report – FY 2002**

Appendix A – FY 2002 Performance Measures and Results

OCC Program	Performance Measure / Customer Service Standard	CY 1999 Performance	CY 2000 Performance	FY 2001 Performance	FY 2002 Target	FY 2002 Performance	FY 2003 Plan
Charter	Average rating of appropriateness of filing location and contact person (Note C)	1.21	1.20	1.20	≤1.5	1.28	≤1.5
	Average rating of overall licensing service (Note C)	1.21	1.17	1.16	≤1.5	1.17	≤1.5
Regulate	Percent of regulations that incorporated plain language criteria	Not Applicable	Not Applicable	100%	100%	100%	Discontinued (Note A)
Strategic Goal 3: Fair access to financial services and fair treatment of bank customers							
Supervise	Average days to process customer complaints and consumer inquiries	45	51	46	50	44	Discontinued (Note A)
Strategic Goal 4: An expert, highly motivated and diverse workforce that makes effective use of OCC resources							
Agency-wide	Percent of planned training completed	Not Applicable	Not Applicable	90%	90%	96%	Discontinued (Note A)
	Statement of Reasonable Assurance under Federal Managers' Financial Integrity Act and Substantial Compliance under the Federal Financial Management Improvement Act is issued	Not Applicable	Not Met	Not Met	Met	Met	Discontinued (Note A)
	Percent of selected capital projects that meet funding, schedule and performance targets	Not Applicable	Not Applicable	100%	100%	100%	Discontinued (Note A)

Appendix A – FY 2002 Performance Measures and Results

NOTES:

A – During FY 2002, the OCC conducted a comprehensive review of its performance measures to ensure they are aligned with the long-term strategic goals and reflect the effect of the OCC's regulatory activities on the national banking system. As a result, many of the FY 2002 performance measures have been discontinued and new performance measures were implemented for FY 2003.

B – The examination survey used for the customer service standards is based on a rating scale of one through five, with one indicating complete agreement and five indicating complete disagreement with the statement about the quality of the examination.

C – The licensing survey used for the customer service standards is based on a scale of one through five, with one representing outstanding, three is neutral, and five represents significantly deficient in rating the licensing services provided by the OCC.

SHORTFALL EXPLANATIONS:

[1] The OCC establishes its annual target for this goal based on the statutory requirement. The OCC achieved 97 percent of its target for ROEs issued to large and mid-size banks. An ROE for 152 of the 157 large and mid-size bank charters was issued during the fiscal year. The OCC waived ROEs for the remaining five charters due to mergers that were in process or other overriding circumstances.

[2] The OCC establishes its annual target for this goal based on the statutory requirement. The OCC achieved 98 percent compliance with the FDICIA-mandated examination schedule for community banks. Mitigating circumstances prevent the OCC from achieving full compliance. For example, the prioritization of resources to higher risk institutions and scheduling anomalies preclude strict compliance with the FDICIA schedule.

[3] Delays in examinations that did not meet the approved exception criteria averaged 17 days. The OCC's managers will continue to monitor and manage the initiation of examinations and limit the length of delays when resources are diverted to problem banks whenever possible.

Appendix B – Glossary

Acronym	Definition
AML	Anti-money-Laundering
CAG	Customer Assistance Group
CMP	Civil Monetary Penalty
COOP	Continuity of Operations Plan
CRA	Community Reinvestment Act
CSRS	Civil Service Retirement System
CY	Calendar Year
DO	Departmental Offices
DOL	Department of Labor
EA	Enterprise Architecture
EFT	Electronic Funds Transfer
FDIC	Federal Deposit Insurance Corporation
FDICIA	Federal Deposit Insurance Corporation Improvement Act
FECA	Federal Employees' Compensation Act
Fed. Reg.	Federal Register
FEGLI	Federal Employees Group Life Insurance
FEHB	Federal Employees Health Benefits
FERS	Federal Employees Retirement System
FFIEC	Federal Financial Institutions Examination Council
FFMIA	Federal Financial Management Improvement Act
FMFIA	Federal Managers' Financial Integrity Act
FTE	Full-Time Equivalent
FY	Fiscal Year
GAAP	Generally Accepted Accounting Principles
GAO	General Accounting Office
GISRA	Government Information Security Reform Act
GLBA	Gramm-Leach-Bliley Act
JFMIP	Joint Financial Management Improvement Program
LMS	Learning Management System
M	Million
MIS	Management Information System
OCC	Office of the Comptroller of the Currency
OIG	Office of the Inspector General
OMB	Office of Management and Budget
OPM	Office of Personnel Management
PAU	Program Analysis Unit
PMA	President's Management Agenda

Appendix B – Glossary

Acronym	Definition
SAM	Self-assessment for Managers
SNC	Shared National Credit
TSP	Thrift Savings Plan
U.S.	United States

www.ingramcontent.com/pod-product-compliance
Lightning Source LLC
Chambersburg PA
CBHW052006280526
45793CB00005B/862

* 9 781505 252156 *